NEW POETRY 5

New Poetry 5

an anthology edited by Peter Redgrove
and Jon Silkin

Hutchinson of London

in association with the Arts Council
of Great Britain and PEN

Hutchinson & Co. (Publishers) Ltd
3 Fitzroy Square, London W1P 6JD

London Melbourne Sydney Auckland
Wellington Johannesburg and agencies
throughout the world

First published 1979

Set in Linotype Bembo by
Input Typesetting Ltd
Printed in Great Britain by
The Anchor Press Ltd and bound by
Wm Brendon & Son Ltd, both of
Tiptree, Essex

British Library CIP data
New poetry.
  5
  1. English poetry – 20th century
  I. Redgrove, Peter   II. Silkin, Jon
  III. Arts Council of Great Britain
  IV. P E N
  821'.9'1408   PR1225
ISBN 09 139570 4

At regular intervals the Arts Council of Great Britain and P.E.N. invite
writers to send in short stories and poems for consideration for
publication in their series of anthologies. Information appears in the
national press, and further details can be obtained from the Secretary,
P.E.N., 7 Dilke Street, London SW3 4JE.

The editors would like to express their gratitude to Sheila Gold, the
Editorial Assistant, for the organization of their work, and for her many
courtesies which immeasurably assisted their task.

Contents

5

Gillian Allnutt

East Anglian Progenitor

My great grandmother
lost the spouse who had walked by her side
coming back from the malthouse
                which was hot
over the wide fields of snow
one night he took pneumonia
and died.

She beat ten children into adulthood.

With a silver crested stick
she tapped her temper to the sticking point
prodded the clods of broad brown fields
to make them productive
wielded the farm on the end of a doughty rod
never took sick but sat up at night
by her furrows of figures
ploughed profit back into the land
made good.

She held each daughter at a needle's end
until she pricked her fingers to the bone
and learned to use a thimble.
And the sons, her favourite ones
                when ripe
were put out to apprenticeship.

She discouraged the doubtful bombardier
who courted the eldest daughter
with a rustle of bombasine
and a stick of a smile
            a spoke
in the broad blue wheeling sky
of his world.

9

          'Toy soldiers' she muttered
churning the milk of motherly love into butter
beating the thousand petticoats to a bloodless white
kneading the bread.

East Anglican, great crested glebe
she drove her brood along the straight road
to the Church doors, stiff with Sunday.
Divers sinful country birds fell quiet.
                        They heard
her stubborn body snap and click over the frozen ruts
and the stick rapped
               to the hard earned glory of God.

Joan Barton

Contents of the Mansion

'Quod habeo teneo'

The General my father had no son.
I am the last. Now all my joints are fixed
and I am living in this servant's room
next to the kitchens to ward off the cold:
I have no patience with 'amenities',
electric current, heating, softnesses;
old Davis once our new-come scullery maid
attends to me and gets the cooking done.
And what I have I hold:

Starting from some mediaeval inmost core
and stretching out in rooms and wings and rooms
as following generations made their mark
this house where I was born bears down on me,
its dull white heavy face outstares the lawn,
the tunnelled yews, the distant landscaped park,
all swept and garnished, shaved and clipped and rolled:
my gardens shall be kept as gardens should.
What I have I hold:

Stacked to the roof with precious artefacts,
Elizabethan beds and corner cupboards,
presses crammed with linen, crewel-work spreads,
and yellowing pillow-lace; priceless I dare say
the tapestries the cobwebs knit together,
the aubussons now fading all to grey;
my lawyers urge these things could yet be sold
to buy a bungalow or hire a nurse.
What I have I hold:

I never cared for reading and have kept
my birthday-present-books as bright as new,
my careful exercises, sums and outline maps,
my mother's copybooks and 'Peep of Day'

11

her 'Struwwelpeter' scribbled on and spoiled;
Rosie my doll in her embroidered dress
dreams in the cradle where she always slept
behind the nursery screen of picture scraps.
What I have I hold:

A gentleman's library behind glazed doors,
Surtees and Syntax, 'The Sporting Magazine',
volumes of pictured fish and brilliant birds,
and sets in tree calf with the crest in gold,
and rosewood desks and Chinese cabinets
stuffed with old letters, diaries, photographs –
shooting parties, the General on the steps,
horses and dogs that go back eighty years.
What I have I hold:

A Worcester service for three-dozen places,
gilt candelabra, coasters, Irish crystal,
china on pantry shelves in due degree
for dining-room and nursery, servants' hall,
the table silver in its velvet cases;
the copper saucepans dulled with verdigris,
old scoops and mortars, leaking jelly moulds,
every cracked kitchen cup, must be preserved.
What I have I hold:

The General's uniforms in pristine splendour
adorn their dummies in the smoking-room
as guardian ghosts of that forbidden quarter,
his dress sword on the wall, Crimean sabres,
and clubs and assegais, and mounted heads,
and guns and rods and moulting salmon flies,
game-books and rusty gaffs, trophies of old
dead wars and of a thousand sporting days.
What I have I hold:

I am the last to bear our ancient crest,
the clenched hand with the motto circling it,
if not by right then as a sacred trust,
the General my father was a long time dying
I cannot reckon now how old I am,

this house where I was born is dust and echoes,
it was a bitter trust he left me to defend:
what if the world is filled with icy shadows
all that I have I hold until the end.

Jane Beeson

Death on Lady Day

The water closets wont flush
Mr Levy wont come.
The best day of the year,
Yes, the best day this year.
'Why dont you
Walk around the garden?'
'The garden?'
'Yes, the garden in the sun.'

'There's an air lock' he said
An air lock?
'The ball-cock' he said,
'Is jammed.'
The finch in the bush
On Lady Day
On Mary's Day
Her son.

'I must wind the clocks' he said
Wind the clocks?
'Yes, wind the clocks' I said
'His wife's taken a message
Mr Levy will come
This afternoon
Soon
In the sun.'

'I've got the map' he said
'The map from the car.
I wanted South-east
But I got South-west.
We'll be back when
Mr Levy
Comes.'

Mr Levy came
In the evening
In the dark.
He went up to the attic
And sought among the boxes
Pushed between the cabin trunks
Sheeted over.

By the night of Lady Day
The closets were flushing
Mr Levy had been
And gone.

James Berry

Nurse Find

Look here now look in a this hut
on chop-chop log –

Granmumma
with no back to straighten up
no good leg to walk
no teeth to bite
not one fowl a yard not even
a rat in a house
or ants a run round the cupboard

Only Granmumma
with three mosquito-leg children

Granmumma
why you so with so-so self
with sun eye a-watch down house top?

How long you sit down here
with children them with so-so place?

How long you sit down here
and no one a-hear God at all
to come and touch you –
you and the children them?

Peter Bland

A Beginning

Guthrie-Smith in New Zealand 1885

Who am I? What am I doing here
alone with 3000 sheep? I'm
turning their bones into grass. Later
I'll turn grass back into sheep.
I buy only the old and the lame.
They eat anything – bush, bracken, gorse.
Dead, they melt into one green fleece.

Who am I? I know the Lord's my shepherd
as I am theirs – but this
is the 19th century; Darwin
is God's First Mate. I must keep
my own log, full of facts if not love.
I own 10,000 acres and one dark lake.
On the seventh day those jaws don't stop.

Who am I? I am the one sheep
that must not get lost. So
I name names – rocks, flowers, fish:
knowing this place I learn to know myself.
I survive. The land becomes
my meat and tallow. I light my own lamps.
I hold back the dark with the blood of my lambs.

Cecily Deirdre Bomberg

Nightmare

Under load,
stumbling and slow
they wind uphill.

And I am there,
the inert onlooker.
They lumber.

How naked the earth has grown
and still not enough wood.
It should be

One man, one cross.
Can wood hold
and earth not split?

Ten palms, ten feet,
five torsos of sweat,
the heads overlapping like monsters.

This one lowers his cross,
the rest pile on.
No struggle.

No guard brutality.
These are the servants of death.
They lie down mute

Under the hammer.
A red thread of blood
binds them together.

Too many men and not enough wood.

Stewart Brown

The Webs

Aimless on my morning walks I find the silk targets,
the tree-rings spun in air;
if all such roundels in my garden are stacked upon each
         other
they form a silver tree, not a birch or willow
but a great silk tree, which you may climb
if you possess the six fingers of a spinner
and the guile of Anansi . . .

A half-breeze rattles the fine webs as a gale whips
         scaffolding
juddering in silver lengths, in rigid glittering waves;
the dew like broken stitches, like knuckle joints of glass.

Stewart Brown

Dead Men's Shirts

Priscilla bought them at a jumble sale,
'a bargain really and I knew you wouldn't care . . .'
Nor do I really, though can't help imagine
what was going on inside these stripes and creases
the last time they were worn.
Knowing what evicted their last tenants doesn't help
but my dear insists; 'That blue one had lung cancer,
this poor chap keeled over with a heart attack,
and that red check belonged to somebody who disappeared
        at sea,
they never found the corpse and rumour is he's done a
        bunk . . .'

I wear these other lives like armour,
know something of them by their taste in shirts
and there's a smell washed deep into the fabric
that persists, though no-one else would notice it.
At first I would hear voices when I pulled them on,
fossil conversations buried in the weft,
could feel resistance to the routine of my dressing,
He buttoned from the bottom, always hung it on a peg,
whereas . . . I sense resentment sometimes, sometimes
        mirth
as if the cloth were in a constant déjà vu,
remembering how the Other One had spent like effort
to no particular end, had frittered time away
on things he knew were unimportant or mere sham . . .

I set to tame the shirts, impose my scent under the arms,
adjust the vents, take up a hem, sew name tags along
        seams

establishing beyond all doubt that they belong to me.
But hung to dry a wind inflates the contours of their pasts,
reveals that other lives than mine still occupy their threads
our separate characters in conflict, now warping to adhere.

Alan Brownjohn

Art Deco Railway Advertisement

It may rain on the crags, but down in the resort
Only a lurking breeze ripples and fans the grey
Nap of the boating lake into pink sunset frills
Like – like scarlet ripples. And now she closes up
Her curtains on their small and disappearing day
With a wan smile, and turns. He sits with one hand warm
From her electric fire, and keeps the other cool
On the smooth rexine flank of the armchair. They dress
Formally, for to-night; and on the sideboard next
The window, on her right, is a neat cut-glass tray
Of sweet aperitifs. I would say she is young,
And something in his eyes makes him the older man.
He focuses the ash-tray on its leather strap
Where he may lately have set down her cigarette:
Nothing has yet deranged its drawn-up thread of smoke,
And all the air they breathe looks hushed, and permanent.
Whatever they may do when dusk has turned to dark
Is hidden from us yet, was hidden from us then;
So all we might conjecture from their perfect pose
– Refined-out versions of what England may have been –
Is that the most she feels concerning his profound
Conviction of her cold, impermeable grace
Is a sympathetic spiritual regard;
And envying their world of carefully-defined
Limits and chances (they need never travel on
To places where correct items of gesture make
No real impression on the bloody flux of things),
I can see reasons why, some forty years ago,
The self I am today should 'Spend a Day in Hove'.

Carol Bruggen

Dear Good Nanny Weetman

We bore the Messiah and hymns. Friday night
was Music night as a rule, but today
Good Friday expunged the sugary Band.
Dear Nanny Weetman grieved for her Lord.

On her wispy head reposed her black straw hat,
a helmet of burnished iron,
cherries hung on the side.

Her quiet look under the fierce gold specs
yielded to laughter every day
but this, an oratorio of glee,
a rush of modest grace.

Suspending her amusement she would save
the family pet, child's prey,
the dangling, wild-limbed dog.

Unruffled with her holy gloves and the pram,
smoothing the baby's pure white curl,
a glazed-eyed fox round her stringy neck
she hushed and whispered the children to church.

Then the polished darning mushroom shone by the fire
and their damp heads steamed in the peace
of that hoarse last shout from the Cross.

She sacrificed her thoughts of fun
and suffered, no kids of her own except
Him at Christmas, the darning of socks, fingers gnarled,
by the hot brass fender in the evening lull.

Her stockings drooping down her thin old legs
above the merciless shoes
she sighed at her tortured corns.

Dear good Nanny Weetman rests with her Lord,
and He submits His savaged brow
to her starchy overall, pure white,
soothed by a biblical non sequitur.

Dear good Nanny Weetman's whitish powdery face,
soft and whiskered and warm,
endured at Passiontide.

Dear Nanny Weetman, censoring stories
so that the good always won hands down,
your flame must flicker somewhere still,
flare in camphorous crannies, glow,

on our small corners your clear pure light reflect
below our cynical shades
in the bloody, despairing dark.

Tom Callaghan

Scenes from a Revolution
(for Roger Howard)

1

'THE REBELS HAVE STORMED THE TOWN HALL':
in the corridor, the clerks count seeds,
scrawl their tallies in the dust.

2

I clutch a chip of marble, torn off
the cathedral tower by some shell.
It cuts into my palm. The veins were broken.

3

'*We* drank a hock, then waited.
No-one in the café was prepared.'
'Wait by the casino door!' she begged.

4

The stem of a wine glass
topples into hawthorn – she is afraid.
'*Six oak, twelve marigold.*'

5

PLEASE IGNORE ALL PREVIOUS WARNINGS.
Leidner's wounds still trouble him:
Paul has trained us all to use the catheter.

6

The Taking Of The City Walls –
'Leave me!' she wept. I said nothing.
'*Seven sycamore, nine willow.*'

7

My car broke down, the driver fled.
Waiting for the troops, gun in hand,
I turn my collar up to face the wind.

8

In the corridors, the clerk counts seeds.
The papers *have* been burnt. Ashes settle.
Towards the horizon, snow shakes, then swells.

Bruton Connors

Memoirs of a Slag Tip

when our father the furnace shot his load
men puddled my conception with iron tongs
with forceps of iron delivered in white heat
the oblong foetus of my brothers
and gave us sweat and often blood
and sometimes their skeleton and total flesh
dropping into us like sparrows
too tired or drunk

they made rails of my brothers and shipped
   them out

but they dumped my foundation on the hill
and built me high and two miles long
like a bull with bloody sides
confronting two towns

they put a train along my cooling back

once I shook it off and trapped the tiny men
in the fire like blood that flowed
down my sides

in the thirties my father the furnace left town

my hide cooled and wrinkled like the moon

the wind gardened my back for hares to nibble
thin lichens sulphuric moss and straws
for ponies and lovers who came and went
and children and gulls make me their arena

and colliers run their rapid hounds
and lice-grey sheep pluck my quills
and vault my orifices my nostrils still warm
from the fire in my lungs

David Constantine

from In Memoriam, 8571 Private J. W. Gleave

Who was at Montauban, Trônes Wood and Guillemont
'So many without memento . . .'

How soon, I wonder, after how many Novembers
    Did the years begin to seem not paces
Interminably around a pit nor steps deserting
    A place, but slow degrees by which she came
Over the curve of the world into that hemisphere
    His face rose in? Again we have given ground;
The dark advances an hour into the afternoon;
    In the interlude between cloud and horizon
A mild sun scythes the field – so by the last winter
    After an illness and before her death
We saw a similar light dawn on the woman
    Who had been a widow more than fifty years.

She lingered in the doorway of the living-room
    Impelled as people leaving are to say
Some word more than goodnight. I have seen her eyes
        shining
    Bright as a young girl's on that threshold
Bright with tears. She found nothing to say. But having
    Her purse in hand – the purse she had kept house from
For generations since the Queen died – she took out
    The new, neat folded notes of her pension
And to the children and their children and their child
    Disposed of these. We do not like to watch
A person look for words nor by whatever gestures
    Taking her leave of table, hearth and chair.

She went to her own room where everything was ready
    To leave, the furniture of her married life
Though in another house, one he had never seen.
    But in that mirror he had seen his face;

They will have stood side by side and looked at
                    themselves,
    She will have stood by herself and remembered.
And always she held the two or three photographs
    Which light had fallen on man and wife to make
In an envelope with the notice of his death
    As if to cross over with these in hand
That she should know him again who had been effaced
    And he should know her who had lived and aged.

By Word of Mouth

Not having seen him die and when
Upon their notification nothing followed
Neither the body to her hearth
Nor any of the late soldier's effects
A little while
As though the outcome could be put in doubt
She trimmed her mourning with a thread of hope
She kept the Suitor from her husband's chair
Showed Death the door
Nightly, until the evenings were long.
He called then with a companion from France.
The neighbours, who miss nothing, saw
Only the soldier leave.

Récit

No messenger in the tragedies
So mean but coming to the wife, the mother
Or any beloved woman waiting
Recounts fittingly the dead man's death
In alexandrines or iambics
And honours him in the telling.
But who the pal was is not remembered
Nor what he said, nor what the questions were
She had the heart to put nor whether
She lamented there and then, praising the qualities
Of the man lost and hiding her face as queens do
In her apron. Not a word, not the place itself
Reached me in his pronunciation
But as to how and where

She only shrugged her shoulders
And perhaps she had that from the messenger
Who did not tell her that the night was very short
And began in a barrage of phosgene gas
And ended in a thick fog
And a barrage of high explosive
As they moved around the southern edge of Trônes Wood
Across seven hundred yards of open ground
Gently sloping to the village of Guillemont
In an attack understood to be hopeless
But serving the French on their right
Whose attack was also hopeless
And that somewhere before the wire
He was obliterated
In gas and night and fog.

★

There being no grave, there being not even one
Ranked among millions somewhere in France
Her grief went without where to lay its head.
She would have rested sooner had she had
Or had she even learned somewhere there was
A well-kept place where he was lying dead.

She could not even think him out of harm:
He must be hurt somewhere by every shell,
Somewhere his mouth could not get breath for gas.
She would have scavenged all his body home
Into the shelter of, if not her house,
At least the roofed and hidden well-walled grave.

But of what comfort is the body home
Which here or there cannot embrace or smile?
And of what comfort is the body whole?
Only the rich and saints do not corrupt.
She almost thought there were degrees of death
And he was more dead piecemeal and abroad.

There being nowhere but the family grave
She went and called her grief out of the air

And coaxed it to alight upon the stone
That did not bear his name. Upon that absence
She grieved as though it were the greater one
And death was lured almost within her view.

She set that feature on the featureless
Visibly everlasting plain of death,
She trod a path, she made some little inroad
And placing three or four remembrance days
She netted in their few interstices
Glimpses that she could bear out of the deep.

★

Like shrapnel in the lucky ones
She carried fragments in her speech
Remarkable to grandchildren
But to herself accustomed
Like rise and shine and left
Left . . . he had a good home and he left
And a long, long trail a-winding . . .

Neil Corcoran

Snow

Makes the slagheap we see from our window
A postcard Austrian alp. It is

A consolation, of sorts, for living
In an English industrial city

In an English industrial winter.
Lights flicker outside, through mist,

And climb the hill like cars,
Fingertipping its braille. We make

A nest for ourselves in here
Of lamplight and books and touch.

Unpin your dress, shake loose your hair,
The world is outside and away,

Its seasons are different from ours:
Time we compute with slowmotion

Movements of skin upon skin, snow
Flaking down on itself as softly

·As lips on a breast, on a thigh,
On the moistening petals of sex,

My hand at rest in your hand.
Unpin your dress, unloose your hair –

Come summer, the alp
Will have long melted back to its slag.

Iain Crichton Smith

On meeting over in Ireland some young poets who write in English

'Feeling,' they said
'that's the important thing' –
those poets who write in English over in Ireland.

It was late.
There was dancing in the hall,
playing of pipes, of bones, of the penny whistle.

They were an island in that Irishness.
'Larkin and Dunn,' they said, 'Now Dunn is open
to more of the world than aging Larkin is.

What room was Mr Bleaney in? It's like
going to any tenement and finding
any name you can think of on the door.

And you wonder a little about him but not much.'
We were sitting on the floor outside the room
where a song in Irish waltzed the Irish round.

Do the stones, the sea, seem different in Irish?
Do we walk in language, in a garment pure
as water? Or as earth just as impure.

The grave of Yeats in Sligo: Innisfree
island seen shivering on an April day
The nuns who cycle down an Easter road.

The days are beads strung on a thin wire.
Language at Connemara is stone
and the water green as hills is running westwards.

The little children in the primary school
giggling a little at our Scottish Gaelic
writing in chalk the Irish word for 'knife'.

To enter a different room. When did Bleaney
dance to the bones? This world is another world.
A world of a different language is a world

we find our way about in with a stick
half deaf, half blind, snatching a half word there
seeing a twisted figure in a mirror,

slightly unnerved, unsure. I must go home.
To English? Gaelic? O beautiful Maud Gonne,
the belling hounds spoke in what language to you?

In that tall tower so finished and so clear
his international name was on the door
and who would ask who had been there before him?

I turn a page and read an Irish poem
translated into English and it says
(the poet writing of his wife who'd died),

'Half of my eyes you were, half of my hearing,
half of my walking you were, half of my side.'
From what strange well are these pure words upspringing?

But then I see you, Yeats, inflexible will,
creator of yourself, a conscious lord,
writing in English of your own Maud Gonne.

Inside the room there's dancing and there's singing.
Another world is echoing with its own
music that's distant from the world of Larkin.

And I gaze at the three poets. They are me
poised between two languages. They have chosen
with youth's superb confidence and decision.

'Half of my side you were, half of my seeing,
half of my walking you were, half of my hearing.'
Half of this world I am, half of this dancing.

Hilary Davies

The Magnolia

She sits, winding the slow coil of her thoughts:
Wire into the brain.
From this place she would hear the bells sing across the
                town
And young men's voices on summer afternoons
Far off from the sanded walks below,
As they went to tea, or bicycled, or were just going
                shopping
For something in town:
Won't be long.

Words guarantors of their return,
Of ritual appointments they would keep,
The sanctity of tea, cricket, dinner
And evenings chosen to be alone,
No tearing at the mind, or time.

Here, rested in her chrysalis-bier, she listened once to their
                world of movement,
Muffled stirring of a country on the other side, uncared
                for, not needed
In her kingdom's soft, dark oyster shell:
No power on earth to make it break before the flood.

Long past the clock had ceased counting the hours –
Never, though she had watched, afraid, had its face known
                change.
Books, chintz window seat, the wide-brimmed hat upon
                the wall
She wove into the splendour of her love's fable,
Herself into a ravelled skein of dreams.

Now, as she curls, she sees still the chapel buttresses push
            straightway to heaven,
Massively rooting their great wings in earth; here, amid
            the season's first flowering,
A magnolia grows, twists on itself,
Squanders its life and bloom in new birth,
Sap running through the wound into beauty:
Silken petals on the grass.

Their blasting has split wide the chrysalis,
Broken her shell, and the shell of the tree's flowers,
What no hand, no sickness nor voyage could do.
The clock strikes: her lover will not come –
She opens now to time, the sun's changing,
Moth stilled for ever in its fragile womb.

Hilary Davies

On Climbing Belas Knap

Under hawthorn heat, spiking wood and barleyfield
With thorns of flame, we climbed;
No skylark but the wind close turning in the trees:
Quiet eddying of time that does not change.

The summer's noonday runs its sleep, swift-fingered,
Through oak and sycamore; a steel-shot web of greenness
Racked tight to the hill's shoulder, pushing bone skywards
In silent aim – all enmeshed are cloud and tussock,
Lilac valley and the poppies, blood-red,
That trace our pathway through the hushing corn.

This is a place of death; grass dips into a long slug of stone
Where darkened orifices still breathe pomp
And blur the windless faces of the grave.
I feel the shadow where my own flesh lies, long-outlawed:
Vanished the rings, the funereal unguents, and gold coin to
            bring
Safe passage into centuries of dreams –
I will make no voyage out across the valley into mist.

My figureheads are broken, split to their powdery core,
While Bela tends his whitening fires and broods:
None come to worship but three alien walkers, and the
            teeming flies.

Jessica d'Este

Song

As
in my mouth
your tongue
full of intention, speaking
not of itself

or
wax, warmed at the wick

melts,

we come
of simple occasions

soft spoken
without conventions
ears, pricked
to listen;

and
stir in flesh
as flesh, stirred
thickens

or
seams to touch

a perfect pelt

of skin, unsplit
of its own breath's fur –

you are myself, done
with difference
or other meaning, being

as if to the wall
from all the world, weeping

drummed
home.

Patric Dickinson

Our Living John

At about page 42 of volume
Two of Moorman's *Life of Wordsworth*,
I was so flooded with his grief
For his brother's death I had to stop
Reading, the words withdrew, I heard
The actual awful sound of John
Drowning in darkness, the uproar on rock,
The turmoil of despair and tempest.

Images for a poem crowded
Unseen, like the impotent rescuers
On the black shore; there, but I neither
Saw them nor gauged them, only felt
Their urgent presence to say comfort
To the dead and living. I went on reading
And by that act dispelled them utterly,

So that when I came to think of those
Suddenly interrupting images,
Nothing on earth could recall them at all,
As if some cock had called back ghosts
To an underworld of the not-yet-living:
Yet there they'd been, felt me, touched me,
But no re-reading of those pages
Could bring their apparitions back.

Like a white frost in spring a full moon
Has left spread on high dalehead
Fields, you wake to see it as the sun
Melts its strangeness, and half a mile
Down the leaprock beck you have to make
Them believe it was no make-believe –
So it was no theatre I was in,
I was there clenched in his raw grief.

So the ship struck hard on the Shambles
And ground itself to bits, grinding
The poet's heart like the grinding of
Glaciers, that will in the end throw up
A sweet fixed landscape with a veri-
fiable past to recollect in,
Wholly unlike the present quaking
Ground the poet stumbles over,

Where sudden springs froth scalding out
Of stone, and fire bursts from the rocky
Tops, and the very sun makes solid
Shadows that endure all night
As hostages for its next rising.
It's always like this, bits of washed up
Bone and timber, no solution,
Centre, comfort in the maze of silence.

– Who can set light to stone,
Who can weep stone tears that yet
Dissolve the monuments they fall on,
Who can feel in the dark
The wordless worldwide ache
For comfort, who so imprisoned craves
But shuns the conditional freedom
Of sleep as a lost time, a lost time to tell –

For months he could tell nothing though
His heart beat on, there was a rift in it
Like a geological fault, an under
Pain, as at Malham Cove in a dry
Spell the water oozes at the foot
Of the cliff, almost still, but after storm
Will leap from the top, so he grieved
Till a storm of tears spouted in a poem.

I was there for a moment living
With him in a black waterfall
That could drown stones. 'He who had been

Our living John, was nothing but a name.'
So he ground the summer suns to cold
Dry dust, whilst insignificant things
All round were prompting his genius to
Weigh again his mortal proportion.

It was an ill time, like a winter
Cuckoo calling in darkness, yet
His greatness made a spring.
                              Let these
Few lines serve as a loving footnote
As to why I had to stop reading
At about page 42 of volume
Two of Moorman's *Life of Wordsworth.*
One of his lives was over.

Mary Dougherty

The Cave Painter

There's no place for an old woman
when she loses her cunning.
Grown more mad than strong I sleep

with the dogs and rise early,
gather my stones,
pound them to powder.

Cow grease thick in my palm
mixes the ochre to paste –
scraped on a slab and carved

precisely into rock.
Pigment and blood sharpen the line
until finally it comes, panting

with wild eyes and horned,
strutting a shaggy flank to my fingers.
And I squat in awe

at the beast of my own life
poised furiously there,
remorseless and stronger than time.

This wall is all that keeps us
when the buzzard and the worm
reclaim their own.

Mary Dougherty

The Burning of Margaret Moone

Something like a rabbit comes
asking me to love it and I answer
the only word I can speak.
Mother.
My body grows perfect.

The balms perfume my temples
and send me swooning.
I wake, scrabble on bent toes,
grow leather wings that horn the night.
Perhaps I am an angel.

I rise like the moon and fly
fierce as an eye through your dreams,
dragging the beaked darkness behind.
Now I fall sidewise
into my shadow.

Each journey leaves me foaming.
All that I am
lays naked on the floor.
Then hands, hands, and my singing stops,
your rack has its own voice.

After a while I forget life.
Flowers of fire grow in my legs,
I lean to the faggots
and flame redeems me.
'Rest now' the tongues whisper.

Then, even as you turn away
I am born.
Even as you hurry toward home,
I wake with my new face
and your daughter's name.

Joan Downar

Sixty Years After

Father's, grandfather's war.
Sepia pictures in popular
histories were what I saw,

and filmed men in awkward
combat rising from mud,
or white sticks frozen hard.

Partly it is the surprise
sweetness of them, their child's
innocence that hurts the eyes;

partly that Tommy and Hun
seem to be fighting some common
enemy that assails them.

Earth turned water is symbol
enough: that Somme and Passchendaele
could liquefy again, now whole.

An old man's war, yet it's
become my memory, not
like many nearer conflicts.

It brings war close, the best
beware of future or past
wars to wear on the breast.

Stephen Duncan

Ospedale

1

Outside in the street a madman calls.
In the hump-backed church next door the sexton waits
for the town simpleton. Slowly along Via Dante
he limps with the ticks of the far-off station clock.

Into the hospital singing porters
carry stiff red pigs on their backs.
The fleshless patients in the ward nod;
drinking bad water has brought me here.
Mafiosi, the old men sit in their pyjamas
in the marble corridor and argue.
Boiled rice they advise and shout at the attendant nuns.

One of them, a giant with hollowed shoulders
comes in and embraces me.
Spluttering in my face, he makes his diagnosis,
his deep sleeves buckets of sickness.

2

Nauseous, the needle drip throbs up my bulging arms.
A merciless cord torture, it drips
alternating answers into me
− I am a heretic, this nurse is a devil
− I am not a heretic, I will believe.

In the night the dimmed light globe
hangs over my head. Rotten, it threatens to split
but sways out through the rain into the mountains:
a huge peach planet.

Jean Earle

The Healing Woman – Of Her Gift

Many keep gardens of herbs
But what comes into me goes beyond herbs –
Nor is it a matter of being called.
Any good neighbour will answer a call,
Taking old skills along
To childbed or sheepfold.

I scarcely heed, at the time, what close-gone thing
Has been chosen to use me –
Only to void the force which, suddenly rising free,
Makes me as a spring tide to swim a fish
Dried up in mud – as a cliff to fall,
Crushing some evil. It is not myself
But that which comes into me.

Afterwards –
If I have gone some way, finding that work,
I can hardly get home.

No one will touch me.

Sometimes my father will come from the house and
            uphold me
In, to my bed. I lie for three days,
Sweating the healed one's darkness out of me.
I can go back then, to cleaning the place. Knitting.
Minding the fowl. Perhaps for long. . . .
It is not every day, nor every year, that God sees
  ·the necessity.

We always live so quiet. It's lonely here.
My father will throw wood on the fire,
Speak to the dog. He has never said
That I ought to get up and cook his supper
Instead of lying there.
And I never ask if he knows what is wrong with me.

Harold Elvin

Holmenkollen

It is Holmenkollen Sunday.

Ski suits, slalom suits, anoraks and sports suits:
kerchiefs, skull caps, devil caps and hoods: ski
trousers, slalom trousers, plus fours and skirts, up
the winding paths to Holmenkollen.

From Stabekk, from Bestun, Sandvika and Jar; from
Nydal, from Gaustad, Besserud and Riis: from Grefsen,
from Grorud, Nitterdal and Skar, up byways and
highways to Holmenkollen.

Cardinal caps, toboggan caps, astrakhans and cowls:
woollen scarves, printed scarves, silk neckerchiefs and
plaids: cardigans, club pullovers, ski kirtles and
coatees, up the forest paths to Holmenkollen.

By steam train, electric train, motor coach and trikk;*
by trolley bus, by autobus, by drosje and by car; by
horse sleigh, by hand sleigh, sparkstötting** and by ski:
up the outlying parts to Holmenkollen.

Through the heart's fat centre, through Akar and
through Town: through the beating pulses, through
Majorstuen and Röa: through the living arteries past
spruces and past fir, up to the classic jump at
Holmenkollen.

Fire reds, shrieking reds, blood reds and wine:
electric blues, navy blues, cerulean and sky: sheet

---

* Electric train-cum-tram.
** A chair on skis.

white, ivory white, ash white and cream, up every track
and road to Holmenkollen.

Men? In dingy grey and liver brown? They must be
there. Somewhere. But it's the women. The women.
In emerald, veridian, verdigris and sea: in sun
colour, sulphur colour, buff colour, gold: in ebony
and ivory, incarnadine and flame: in every shouting
tone to Holmenkollen.

Karl has called for Signé, and Hans has called for Anne.
Kristian's called for Inger, and Sebastian for
Liv: and half are eating sausages on their way to
Holmenkollen.

Olaf, Otto, Konrad, Karl; Axel, Ivaar, Martin, Max;
Torsten, Jonas, Steinar, Sten: are somewhere on the
road in their ski-club pullovers and their topplue
hats, with their clasp knives at their belts and their ski-wax
handles. Their fathers all wear astrakhans,
elkskin boots and gaiters: their mothers all wear
woollen hats and coats of seal or reindeer: but their
sisters, 'ah! their sisters!' flood the stream in
colour and monopolize the scene.

Arnold Blake has left his home three miles to the
west. He's kicking his heels down Griniveien staring
at the birches on the way and at the red berries still
clinging to the mountain ash.

Roland's called for Einar and they drink last cups
of tea and hastily prepare their smörbröd and their
pilsner for the day. Soon they too will be swallowed
in the blood-stream.

Magda's called for Sofie.

Hundreds are now gathering in the horseshoe, by the
place where the lake lies frozen: hundreds champ the
thick snow on the hills. The reserved seats are yet
untaken and the members' stands unfilled: but the

53

brass band is assembling on the rostrums. Norwegian flags are flying, some Swedish and some Finnish: and the King's box rises up to meet the sky. The great shoot itself rises in the west and stands away from people unattached. Soon its favourites will be sweeping down its slope and from its sudden tip-up end plunge out headlong at the crowd.

Green are the spruces that fold round the theatre; ash blue is the sky overhead. White is the snow that lies on the tracks and royal the blue on the stands. But outside; outside the stands, among the crowd itself; outside the arena, is a kaleidoscope in spectrums.

Roland and Einar are on their way moving in a human artery up Blindernveien.

Arnold Blake has finished staring and has joined a human wall up Ankerveien.

Magda and Sofie scramble out and in past pine and birch: and Magda can't stop humming and Sofie can't stop laughing.

Up Bogstadveien and Slemdalsveien; up Dronningsveien and Holmenveien; up Stasjonsveien and Frognerveien; up every dirt and concrete road to Holmenkollen.

From the mink farms out at Godthap, from the schaefer homes at Bogstad, from the wood-mills by Lake Mardal, by ski, by sleigh or on the foot to Holmenkollen.

'Hot dogs! Hot dogs!'

Gibble-gabble, bibble-babble, chatterbox verbosity; jabbering and prattling, effervescing, flippancy: snow-balls at every blonde, and snow-balls down the neck 'whow! that's cold!'

'Hot dogs! Hot dogs!'

Arvid walks with Ellen, and Harald walks with Else;
Thorleif and Arnald are chasing Gerd and Gunhild:
Magnus Karlsson, Thorleif Sandberg and Petter Henricksen
have joined a score of others and clasping hips are
walking like a serpent up to Holmenkollen.

'Hot dogs! Hot dogs!'

Cream and blue, cream and blue, stand out in
predominance and smear the forest paths of Nordmark
in the national tones of Norway.

Men? You can see them here and there if you
stare with hard set eyes: but one young blonde in
some stark living colour will blot out ten of them.

The mothers take the sandwiches, the brothers take
the flasks: the fathers take the tickets . . . but it's
the sisters, it's the sisters, that flood the woods
with colour and set the snow aflame.

'I say,' said Roland.

'Yes ol' man?'

'This is rather fun. I have been in football
crowds in London, at the Arsenal and West Ham, I've
seen Wolverhampton in the final games at Wembley,
and though every one is happy, excitable and kindly,
their colours are all fading and their greys and
browns are dead. Yet here the crowd is different,
no jollier no brighter, but this feast of colour
floods me through and makes me feel so good.
"Whoopee!" '

'Hot dogs! Hot dogs!'

And he grabbed a bunch of spruce and shook two feet
of snow upon the wonder heads of two blue-eyes
Norwegians.

And Roland and Einar and two ash Viking blondes are walking up together in the living stream of people, in the rushing flood of colour, in the busy beating arteries that feed this heart of Norway on this Holmenkollen Sunday.

Ricky Emanuel

Mrs Greedy & the Pigs

She put the pig on a spit and
warmed it till the hooves
were varnished with dripping and the mouth barked
with the last croak of its enormous
going from ordure, look, it
said, Mrs Greedy, you are doing this
to revenge the portent
of your own eventual
demise. She ate it
on Sunday crunching
the stoved outer covering
that lit the porcine chins of her young
whose penultimate sibling, gestating beyond the os
a little open and idiotic with use,
sopped up the gobbets for the
making of the hair on its chinny
chin, little pig little pig let
me come said the anointed Mr Greedy.

Ricky Emanuel

A Death

A great woman,
newly come to husbandry, is lit with the passion
of having slain a sheep! she said how
in truth they are meek, on sticking
it keeled over without uttering a sound
and now's stripped, hanged from her pantry ceiling,
of all its back woollens. Sheep die nobly, she said,
unlike pigs who screech every last ounce
of the bright wonderful liquid
for her pudding. I thought she would look good
herself on a hook,
magenta ham, marbled with boiling,
the breast, haggis, sagging,
her enormous poundage larded
across the good housekeeping memorandum.
If her fat could spit
for breakfasts it would leach
out of me all of the violence she engenders;
and such meekness would leak in,
such a warm gruel of loving
for my new neighbour, such a vegetable
pottage of kindness!

Gavin Ewart

Sestina: The Literary Gathering

At one end of the peculiar table Jeremy
sat, and talked about poetry to Carl.
He was a bit of a nutter. Next to him, Sheila
was eating a farinaceous dish. Lewis
listened intently to the words of Ursula.
They were all drinking cider. And so was Jane.

There was something quiet and achieved about Jane –
of course she was a good deal older than Lewis –
and she hadn't got the manic quality of Jeremy
nor did she understand engineering, like Carl,
or the details of catering, which obviously Ursula
had at her fingertips. They all liked Sheila.

They all agreed there was no one like Sheila
for lovability. Music to Jeremy
was the breath of life. Often, to Carl,
he would play his autoharp – this delighted Ursula
and certainly caused some pleasure to Jane –
sitting in the meadow with the cows and Lewis.

'Lewis?' said Jane. 'He's a dark horse, Lewis!'
'You never know what he's thinking!' cried Sheila.
'He's a very nice boy' was the verdict of Ursula;
he seemed more ordinary to Carl and Jeremy.
He was fond of Milton (he once told Jane) –
but only modern poets appealed to Carl.

There was a hint of dark Satanic mills about Carl,
a contained intelligence; no fly-by-night Jeremy,
he hadn't the open character of Ursula,
in this respect he was more like Jane
or the sheep and the cattle. And only Sheila
seemed to understand him – except for Ursula.

59

There was a bardic bravery about Ursula.
Not even Lewis, or Jane, or Sheila
had her bravura – in the words of Lewis
'She is the mother of us all!' For Jane
Ursula's writing was the tops, and Carl
confessed he was staggered, and even Jeremy,

though he liked Carl and respected Jane
and admired Lewis (and the work of Sheila),
said how he, Jeremy, really worshipped Ursula.

Ruth Fainlight

The Function of Tears

The function of tears
must be to serve as language,
a message to others –
yet the bitterest weeping
takes place alone. The message
then for oneself, an urgent
attempt to reach
that shackled prisoner
in the deepest dungeon
far below the level
of the lake.

What do tears express
that words cannot do better?
Tears are the first language –
a glazed face and anguished
moans communicate
rage, pride, regret;
pleasure or frustration;
remorse and hatred;
almost every emotion
sufficiently intense,
before words can be formed.

Each of these feelings
in turn must colour
the soul of the prisoner
abandoned in her corner,
like the shifting greys
tinged by rainbow hues
of light filtered
through tears clogging
her lashes, jagged
prisms of memory

and hope in the gloom.

Such tears have little effect
on the silent warder
who checks the links
of her chain, brings bread
and drinking water
and sometimes even
changes the musty straw.
No-one has ever seen
the warder cry –
not his wife or children,
not the torturer.

Perhaps the lake
was hollowed out by tears.
But until the castle
is assailed, besieged,
completely undermined –
with dungeons flooded,
crenellations tumbling –
and torturer, warder,
and prisoner are forced
to shout above the sound
of rushing water,

call to each other for rescue,
swim clear of the ruins,
embrace and cry with relief,
that lake, like the socket
of a giant eye drowned
by unimaginable
grief, will still stare
blindly up towards heaven
and go on weeping,
endlessly replenished
from a fountain of tears.

Martyn A. Ford

Roosting

The Adulterer, Grown Old, Remembers

At four o'clock the elms around the pond
Hiss with starlings. Their cloak's in tatters now,
You can see right through it to Kemptown.
It's rather like the big clear-out after a death,
When you come across some faded ball gown,
Twitching with tiny moths, and hold it up
And see the light of winter stabbing through.
But I recall their bodiless seething,
Like some wild rumour,
Unexplained and deeply unsettling, one summer,
Walking here with somebody else's wife.
No ordinary indiscretion – the mad breathing
Of that last endless evening, passing into night.
Now, I am afraid, November's blown our cover
– Ours and the starlings';
Ever and always the season insists its lesson:
That age lays bare the folly of a lover,
And in cold winter come no more dears and darlings
Under the ragged elms,
But a white-haired lady, with her dress on,
And a nice old gentleman, keeping to the paths.

Robin Fulton

Undated Photograph

The dead had the whole world to themselves then.
Brahms leans, uncomfortably
close to tipping over, less kempt
than the tied leafless creeper on the wall.
He looks at me as if I weren't there.
He must have stared at me a moment before
getting up and finishing his life.

In his own good time of course. It's this
photo that hurried off through space,
eighty years later? reaching me
like today's news. And on. News that'll still
be news in the twenty-first century.
Like a generous miracle it leaves
a fair copy of itself in my brain.

In silence. What of the black notes lying
untidy as seeds in closed pages,
in the dark where no-one can read
or hear them? All they can do is wait.
I think of arctic lupin seeds once
found after ten thousand years
in ice – unabashed, they rooted and flowered.

That's extreme. Someone must be playing
Brahms somewhere, always, another extreme,
his music a rare element in the air.
Look, his hands are stiff as dead wood.
Look, as the ash fell from his cigar
and invisible preparations were made
for a new season's crowding weeds.

Roger Garfitt

Homage to James K. Baxter

Despair is the only gift;
When it is shared, it becomes a different thing

James K. Baxter, from *Runes*
posthumously published by Oxford University Press in 1973

A newsagent taking in the first papers
would see us taking shape at the counter,
the ghost trade, come for Mars and Old Holborn, sugar
    and smoke.

Each morning, a shortchanging of the shadows,
as they rose from areas and stairwells,
sleepless from skinpopping methedrine.

Ah! the nights on the road
on a mattress, 'on the move' through
the bleak indoors. Joe Tex sang of

stogies as we rolled our Social Security
into straights, played *Indianapoly* through the small hours:
the speed kings, firing on half an amp.

And yet it was almost good, to be one
of a tacit company, to be men without women,
low lifeforms in a basement room.

Only. a few of us became serious ghosts.
Our selves shadowed us. Only the present
can be lost in Lethe,

as I would lose it now, for your company.
But the light breaks. And already the shapes
are forming at the counter.

Jon Glover

Letters and Fictions

One in America, the rest now scattered
or dying here by the shore, the recovery of love
seems beyond any task permitted by hunger and cold.
God knows, I believed no one could just go.
The world was not to be trifled with.
I was a tenant and obedient to the will of the place.
Though still I thought my love crossed enough
                    boundaries.
And now his journeys consume my present,
and his past is freed, cancelled rather,
by each new marvel. He describes flowers in such
                    profusion
I think he is mad. Paradise? It wasn't promised
for the price of a voyage. The sea and the land are work,
work and death, and as for love
all I want is to finish it and sleep.

'I saw enormous lilies. They were red and gold.
The summer sun is so bright I could not believe
nature could go on matching it, radiance for radiance.
Orchards, wheat-fields and the rich, cracking mud.
The smell of heat. Who needs to praise God
amongst this opulence? I met a painter who simply
records what is there: orchids, poison-ivy and
the humming-birds no Northerner has seen.
This observation, again and again is love.
My senses grow, and desire.'

Now the village is burnt, his letters will have no answer.
They become fictions.

Jon Glover

Nature

I stop for hours to watch butterflies. I am tempted not to draw them but to collect them. Sometimes I think I would like to watch them grow and breed. Then I fancy arranging them, to kill and preserve their abundance, their colours, their alien delicacy. Still I have nowhere for this. And, finally, to set things in a house would create a stillness shut from the sun, a civilization that I go on trying to leave.

From earth colours and its skin
of thin, dry crystal,
its fragile liquids snap out and are gone.
Without tenderness
or anything sensual
it holds my gaze, meets food,
flower or parasite
across void after void:
the blank spaces come
and go on coming.

Touching their fine dusts
tempts me to indifference –
all those designs, fantastic eves,
and mimicked leaves grow
without fear or knowledge,
display purpose and beauty
without love and die raggedly
or freeze. These human qualities
want them collected, row upon row,
preserving each as a separate
kingdom of man's desire?
Like cold, pinned galaxies?

W. S. Graham

The Alligator Girls
(Remembering Crowe Ransom)

Are you to tell me where my soul is cast
Or in an alligator or a god.

Or would you like to bring the girls at ransom
Over to have a picnic beside the sweet
Clear water. This is the very day for it.
Bring your apricot over. Tell the girls
The mill is off and to come on over
And we'll all put our toes in the sweet river.

An afternoon by the river with two sisters
Is something special. We shouted Gator Gator
And out came May and Bonnie lifting their skirts
Prancing with mock terror out of the shallows
To lovingly berate us. That was when
I worked in America as a young man.

I am told the river had alligators in it.
May and Bonnie are grown up and dead.
But we had some great fun, didn't we?

W. S. Graham

A Page About my Country

Quhen Alexander the king was deid
That Scotland haid to steyr and leid,
The land sax year, and mayr perfay,
Lay desolat efter hys day.

And that is John Barbour making
'The Bruce'. Dunbar came later, A'
Enermit else as the language
Changed itself from beast to beast.

Where am I going to speak tonight
And in what accents? Apprentice me
To Scotland I said under the hammer
Headed crane of Harland and Wolfe
Who were very good to my father keeping
Him on. We did not need to go
Down into the Lyndoch Street soup kitchen.
I am only telling you. It does not matter.
Dad, are we going to the Big Dam?

Curlew. The curlew cried flying
Crookedly over lonely Loch Thom.

Quhen I came headlong out to see
The light at the top of the land
At One Hope Street spitting the hairs
Of my mother out, to tell you the truth
I didn't know what to do. The time
Was five o'clock the bright nineteenth
Of November nineteen-eighteen.
The time is any time to tell
Whoever you are the truth. I still
Don't know what to do. Scotland?

A word meaning an area and

Here I see it flat pressed
On my Mercator writing table.

Look I am looking at my sweet
Country enough to break my heart.

MacDiarmid's deid under a mound
O literature making no sound.

And Mars is braw in cramasie.

Teresa L. Gray

Memories Across Dead Ground

We travelled the shore road and none went on before –
Three yards from the salt weed where the long water came
Lapping at the quiet land as a deer might come
And white in sunlight stood the bony hills of Clare.
We went past the white farm and the haymaking,
Their white horse from Connemara and the helpers,
Aproned Mother, Nun on leave, the Son, the Father
And bonnetted children busy at their raking.
No sound (and all here's tumult) save a dripping oar
Mirrored on crystal air and one voice over water.
Grass here bends from the wind of bombs and the thrown
       flame
And white in sunlight stand the bony hills of Clare.

Frederick Grubb

Rite of Spring

A long journey, why.
Slept through orchards maybe,
Then station smog. Sleep an odd

Response to longing. You drove to a house
Next day drove
Further north. The Cheviots engender

A faded, ancient blue, in budding spaciousness
And frail emphatic line
Of Lindisfarne, envenomed by intense

Spray, the holy island. No fear
Of Danes landing near
These fishing villages.

On quays, past painted doors, we strolled.
It's clear your son
Has your glance, your laugh, your voice

At four years old.
A castle puts muscle in
The estuary's elbow: you explain the chapel:

Arrowed arches in the Durham style.
Soprano of birds rang through that ruin
Like the rule of law, the rite of spring.

Your black hair
Distant and precise, you face the horizon
Whence the Danes might sail, and I

Half expect
White, but like the first and last
Sight of a lifetime

You stand by rocks, gulls floating
Into the eye of the waves. One has to say
Be as you are, do not be otherwise, we have

No other means to living in the present.
Fugitive, the black
Gull dives, not tragic, but apart.

The beauty of its trajectory is true.
This love is what I have
And it escapes me.

Chris Hardy

The Crop

Beneath the Planes lie
their seeds, on the paving stones.
The trees are grey and large
hauling water through a well
in the pavement. They have
blotched, sickened faces
being out all night
like ageing, fervent
pleasure seekers.
London Planes,
a rank of wooden cobwebs,
when did they have
their own nature?

It's not surprising.
From Lavender Hill the vale
of Thames beneath, full
of trees, cushioning the weight
of stone bonded
far northward.
In this Human world
everything is under arrest.
The Planes make one effort
to be free: At night,
people sleep, few cars yet
to crush the crop, dropping
in the dark.

June Ella Harris

Midsummer

Far
inland
hot sun
reminds
me of
childhood's
beached
days.

The sea
rinses
my patio.

Caught
in its
swell
is a
starfish

no bigger
than a
baby's hand
spread out
to dry.

Tony Harrison

Next Door

from 'The School of Eloquence'

1

Ethel Jowett died still hoping not to miss
next year's *Mikado* by the D'Oyly Carte.
For being her 'male escort' (9!) to this
she gave my library its auspicious start:

The Kipling Treasury. My name. The date:
Tony Harrison   1946
in dip-in-penmanship type copperplate
with proper emphases on thins and thicks.

Mi mam was 'that surprised' how many came
to see the cortège off and doff their hats –
All the 'old lot' left gave her the same
bussing back from 'Homes' and Old Folk's flats.

Since mi mam dropped dead, mi dad's took fright.

His dicky ticker beats its quick retreat:

It won't be long before I'm t'only white!

Or t' Town Hall's thick red line sweeps through t' whole
         street.

2

Their front garden (8 × 5) was one of those
the lazier could write off as 'la-di-dah'.
Her brother pipesmoked greenfly off each rose
in summer linen coat and Panama.

Hard-faced traders tore her rooms apart.
Litter and lavender in ransacked drawers,
the yearly programmes for the D'Oyly Carte.
'Three Little Maids' she'd marked with '*4 encores!*'

Encore! No more. A distant relative

roared up on a loud bike and poked around.
Mi mam cried when he'd gone and spat out: '*Spiv!*'

I got Tennyson and Milton leather-bound.

The Sharpes came next. He beat her, blacked her eye.
Through walls I heard each blow, each *Cunt! Cunt! Cunt!*

The Jowetts' dahlias were left to die.

Now mi dad's the only one keeps up his front.

3

All turbans round here now, forget flat caps!

They've taken over everything bar t' CO-OP.
Pork's gone west – chitt'lins, trotters, dripping baps!
And booze 'n all if it's a Moslem owns t' new shop.

Aye, t' Off Licence, *that's gone Paki in t' same way!*
(You took your jug and bought your bitter draught)
I can't get over it, mi dad'll say,
smelling curry in a pop shop. Seems all daft.
Next door but one this side's front room wi t'
Singers *hell for leather all day long 's*
some sort o' sweatshop bi the looks on it
running up them dresses . . . them . . . sarongs!

Last of the 'old lot' still left in your block.
Those times, they're gone. The 'old lot' can't come back.

Both doors I notice now you double lock –

He's already in your shoes, your next-door black.

Tony Harrison

Stately Home

'Behold Land-Interest's compound, Man & Horse'
(Ebenezer Elliot)

Those bad old days of 'rapine and of reif!'
Northumberland peles still seeping with old wars:
this year's lawful lord and last year's thief,
those warring centaurs, scratch their unscabbed sores.

But here, horned koodoo and okapi skulls,
the family's assegais, a Masai shield,
the head of one of Chillingham's white bulls,
this month's *Tatler*, *Horse & Hound*, *The Field*.

Churned earth translucent Meissen, dusted Spode
displayed on Sundays for the pence it makes,
paintings of beasts they'd shot at or they'd rode,
cantered grabbed acres on, won local stakes,
once all one man's debatable demesne,
a day's hard ride from Cheviot to sea –

His scion, stretching back to Charlemagne,
stiff-backed, lets us put down 40p.

Nora Holding

Proceedings of a Member
of the Society

One day last month searching for specimens
along a lonely shore, riding the waves
a few yards out I saw a log or small
tree-trunk: this I reclaimed. Some shells, attached

in clusters to the sodden wood, I found
to be a form of Lepas anatifera:
atypically these shells were luculent.
Of them I collected five. Opening

afterwards the four of smaller growth, amazed,
in each I found, secured by a membrane
at the beak and claw, a bird, half-fledged. As
in a dream I found the book, turned up the

page and read 'The Shell half-open and the
Birde ready to fall out which no doubt were the
Fowles called Barnacles' . . . So this was madness –
to see what was not – see and touch and feel . . .

I looked towards the bench – it might be bare –
I sane. And the last shell had opened – this
the largest one. There was a tiny goose –
I judged less than eight centimetres beak

to tail – perfect in all its parts; adult
in plumage: black cap and neck, white face, brown
irides, black legs and tail. Swiftly, it ran
towards the window – I ran too – not fast

enough – it flew upwards and out. I crushed
the other shells, like cracking nuts, two in
each hand – the splinters pierced my flesh – I felt
and heard the small bones break – I dared not look –

then threw the mess outside. I washed, sat down
to write my notes, began 'The tribe Caridea,
including the prawns and shrimps of our own coasts' –
I moved my hand: there was a smear of blood
across the page. I put my pen down. Wept.

Frances Horovitz

Quanterness, Orkney 3500 BC

Not blood, but fact, from stones and the sieved dust.

'*Most die at twenty*'
  – syllables snatched by wind.
Died of bone's ache, belly's ache,
  the ninth shining wave,
or long attrition of the absent sun.
'*Before the Pyramids, this death-house
was the centre of their lives.*'
Equal in death,
man, woman, young and old,
laid out for carrion, their wind-scoured bones
heaped hugger-mugger in the corbelled dark.
'*Some rodent bones were also found.*'

Each desperate spring
winds drift flower-scent from off the sea;
lambs call like children.
In warm heather
the young lie breast to breast
seeding the brief sun into their flesh.

Womb-hunger to outlast the stones.

Frances Horovitz

Sea-horse

Holiday trophy from Cornwall
he lies in cotton wool, fingernail long.
Obsidian eye glitters.
He is light as a husk, fragile.
Embryo perfect
he seems not dead, but waiting.

My son weeps at his strangeness;
Pegasus and mermaids are more familiar.
Except in dreams we do not remember
his watery meadows,
the undulant winds of his prairie.
Is it accident we bring him here
to limestone hills?
Creatures of his kind rise patiently
age after age toward the air,
the spade fragments them,
we kick them up at every step.
Certainly, thrown out as junk,
he will become dust with them,
his particles will ride the fields in summer air
— a resurrection, briefly, into light.

Roger Howard

Wolves' Wood

1

One step nearer,
I will not let the blade slip.
Beetles in the bark
tap and hold out,
I listen to their hard dialect,
it grows harder.
Elder is brittle and smells bad
yet heals,
oaks support galls,
I remove the dead limbs
of hornbeams.
The beetles leap, twist and fall.
In the ivy, in their hole,
owlet
squashes against owlet.
I cut right back
to the stump.
I say to my dog,
'Clear acre, bare coppice,
three years' growth
brings ten nightingales.'

2

In the thicket
a blackcap sings,
round and round the birches
redpolls wheeze,
I am no wiser.

I avoid holly,
I put my nose
in guelder rose,

hands and neck itch.
'Don't scratch.'

3

In the wood's centre
my dog digs
yet another circle,
a hole with its paws
in the war's crater.
I climb down
the dark depression,
up to my knees
in leaves swept there
by the wind.
I bend and take
from her wet jaws
a part of what bomb,
sticky with saliva?

4

Spring comes unasked,
I don't trample
on purple orchid,
I make my way round
a pond full of crowfoot.
I let the jay
suck thirteen eggs
in the wren's nest I guarded.
I filled the holes of badgers,
smoke made my eyes smart.
I watched voles play,
their thin cries
were too loud for my ears.
I lied to the elm
it was not dying.
In the deep thicket
I walk into gloom.
At the top of the alder
I eat seeds.
For the roe deer there's

a way through Wolves' Wood.
Eyes down
I follow the hoofprints.

Michael Hoyland

Speed

An hour before spruce Lance lay kissing
The veined slime in Scultrupps brook
   He touched his wife,
   Stepped with his samples to his Ford
   And rushed through arcs of light
   For London.

His mouth pressed the stream three weeks,
His suit ran green.
The car, crushed like a bucket and rusting,
Settled to its seats.
   His samples, burst by the rain,
   Sold nothing.

Paul Hyland

Jerusalem Zoo

*'They shall not hurt or destroy in
all my holy mountain.'*

Isaiah 11.9

In Jerusalem they are forcing God's hand.
Cages, high fences enable paradise
inside them; or will, when what the Zoo has planned
is brought to pass with all the stoic purpose
of Dispersion gathered to possess the land.

In Cage One, strange bedfellows, lambs with the wolf;
in Two, leopard and kids. Rank fur rubs fleece.
In Three and Four, the lion preens himself,
the bear walks on hind feet; they nuzzle grass
with skittish comrades, the fatling and the calf.

Eden behind bars. Replenished earth subdued.
Pilgrim and sightseer, Arab and Jew will press
wide eyes and lenses at Isaiah construed
with exact pedantry. To haste Messias
a baby in Cage Five crawls on the asp's brood,

a weaned child puts his hand on the adder's den.
Apart, at night, the prey chew cud. Predators
rend red meat, gorge in the old tradition.
So is the new day filled with docile creatures
and, to be realistic, model children.

Small cages. Man still at large, who paused to weep
over Jerusalem, astride a young ass
rode over strewn garments, crowds' applause, their hope
pinned to a cross. He must repeat that progress,
bars must burst, and the millenium escape.

Trevor Innes

Family Communion

Branwell

Black spume like cannon shot. Fountains of steam.
At Luddenden the new age shunted by him.

Unfinished, his oil-streaked visions would not last,
Flaked and creasing, opaque with shadow.

And last evening's stupor left his mind blank,
Hung-over in the gathers
Of cold clear air.

The ticket – punched and labelled.

If only he had a memory
To bank his heart around

He would die happy!

Emily

Hurrying so,
Her bonnet leant into the wind,
As swift as her tiny boots would carry
(How could she go faster?)

In the eye of the tempest
Massed black and gathering, from Lancashire,
And, behind, the wide Atlantic

To bend where burnt sienna
Sluices a sheer rock culvert,
Marl bared and upfolded,

   long-cooled from the earth's hot heart,
And flints where tussocks grit and hold their station.

Where her lord would come

Or would not come.

Why should she have to say this?

Charlotte and Mr Nicholls

Trying to smile once she caught her face
In his mirror, her best profile,
But the mouth sharp and thin, the eyes cold.

Straightening her last possessions
Months later he was caught
By the engravings of Lord George Gordon
And the brooch from her father she never wore,
Black as jet,

Made of jet,

And he remembered,
With a tremor in his jowls, bewhiskered,
How the cobbles and gravestones danced
In the hard thin rain again
That morning, when they broke
Bread for the last time, man
And wife and 'child-to-be'.

The Reverend Patrick

From the holy land of Ireland
Picked out as one of the likely
And collecting a French name
He came
To the parish chosen for its sins

And climbed to the churchyard siding the rectory
Where bacillae leaked from the crowds of scrubbed corpses
Streaming through strata, down Main Street gunnels,
For decades in a soiling cycle.

But this was the only promised land
With its whipped congregation, scab-faced and bloody,
Wastrels and whores, pursuing the horses and easy virtue,
Going to hell with their eyes wide open.

An iron will and privacy it needed,

He thought, locked in study
At the top of the stairs at the top of the hill
Till
His focus clouded.

His children's keeper,
He kept repeating
   'What is the best book?
   And what the next best?'

And bowing to God and Nature only
His true flock trailed through the cold wet house,
Their matins and vespers. Our Father

Who laid out time and suffered
No other.

He gave them that freedom and that love.
And that denial. The daddy of them all!

Jenny Joseph

The Inland Sea

Did I tell you of a strange dream I had?
I was in the upper country, mule country,
The track twisting, dust, stone; sometimes,
Standing rare and beautiful, a thistle
On a cliff edge. White sky behind it.

Suddenly, singing
Was coming up the valley; and as it neared –
The little group – you could see that it travelled with
            them –
The green carpet of the valley floor:
Grasses and fronds with hanging heads, and mosses.

The fore man stood by me on the cliff
A Chinese ivory sage that fits in the palm
With every thousand hair in his beard distinct
And wrinkles lining a face as smooth as a pebble
But complete and whole; and this man spoke to me.

'It is the inland sea we seek,' he said
'And we will journey ever,' and round the mountain,
As they moved on like a shoal in the ravine bottom,
Winding as one, like a cloud across the sky,
Their distant singing swayed and ebbed with the wind
And I felt safe because these old men sought
The inland sea.

I remember a girl telling me
(Brown curly hair, fresh skin and open eyes
Sweet honest and innocent English abroad –
I don't think they are made like that any more –)
Of her meeting the man that she was now engaged to.
They had met and she dreamt that she was married to him
And the second time she saw him told him her dream.

91

She was not bold or fishing or plotting consequence.
'Wasn't it strange' she'd said 'to have such a dream?'
And he asked her to marry him.

Why do I, a life-time late, these years after
Talk of dreams, fabricating premises
When we both know it may be so or no
And not matter; when the direct truth
And the direct lie are muddied by convenience
And compromised;
When all is a game we would like to win, but know
The losing will shake us for only a little while
Before we slip back into our haze of self
Where all is slumber within wired-up walls?

Why? Listen. Come a little closer, near as you dare
To the edge of this spur. The soil's a little crumbly
But there are hawthorns, sloes and other bushes
Knitting the escarpment. Here is shade
And safety on the edge of danger. A place I found
By long trekking, retreating at times with care
Not to loosen rock, and going about
Another way until I found this nest.
Listen. Inch forward. What do you hear in the wind
That, freed from the bluffs, is meandering with the river?
Look up to the sky an instant, do you not see
Immense lakes of light lying within the clouds?
Part these grasses: spread out fair below
The hidden, ancient, still-fructifying source
Silent shines in sunlight.
Can you see? Come a bit nearer then. Now.
Look: we have come to the inland sea.

Richard Kell

Four Poems from *Heartwood*

The Rescue

Gentle, warm, dark, the sea
you rocked her in; dreadful
the fire your love became
to give her breath. But once
wasn't enough, it seems:
what providence conceives
a crux like this? – the child
delivered into pain,
you strangling in warped floods,
the labour of your birth
into final stillness.

The Scattering

Ashes . . . What else?
A breath for new lovers
climbing Killiney Hill?
A clear harmonic in some timeless music?
Or, miraculously, your self
distilled from all you were, knowing for ever
'I', and even 'thou'? So many voices.
One, echo on echo, keeps saying
'Ashes, what else.'

Working Late

(*The City of God*, Bk XII, Ch 7)

Silence is my self all round me.
Once it was good, because I knew
you were curled in the bed upstairs,
that I'd sleep to the rhythm of your
breathing, and we'd wake together

93

gladly, loving and undeceived,
allies against our sliding wills.
Now it is full of your absence,
the worst silence I've ever been –
charged with nothingness, implying
more than Augustine's dark logic.

But I know the other half still,
the tide rising: even the heart
of a silence mortal as this
can be redeemed: our children lie
sleeping upstairs, their lives my trust
renewed at each lonely waking.
Nothingness lapses too: a breath
of being fills the long small hours.

Marriage Is Like a Tree

After the flood, its roots are dying in air.
When twenty-two rings of tough growth
fell in a race of water,
the bark was lumpy with healed wounds,
the heartwood sound.

I recall, with a love that's inward now,
its many changes: foliage playing
in light, drooping in damp glooms
or stilled by rich calms of summer;
branches furred with snow, or their stormy thrashing.

How sad, these emptied places. But elsewhere
you find, again with sadness, trees that were hurt
too deeply, unnerved by pest and fungus,
hollowing to their last stand
against the rising wind.

It could be a kind of luck, being left
the ghost of a scarred tree
still healthy when it toppled:
leaves whispering through all the mind's seasons,
a root safe in the ground for ever.

Frank Kelly

Hometown or 'Where We Won The War'

Having no alternative, we choose a place — and learn to live.
And having learned — how, or why, choose somewhere else to
learn to die?

'Print your address,' said Sister Thérèse, 'just as on the
        letters that
the postman brings.' So Joe Ryan wrote, 'heep street
        bratford finel notis'

'That's the mill where we won the war,' said Uncle Ed, a
        shop steward
who spent his war trying to start strikes — and the peace
        preventing them.

A broad, yellow stain of horsedung down the middle of
        the street
vanished in the rain but instantly came back at the first
        gleam of sun.

Horses brought everything — the rag-and-bone-man's
        pennies; coal in sacks;
milk ladled out of steel churns; oak-barrelled beer to the
        corner pub

— The Cock And Bottle — 'All we're up against!' said
        Father Murphy, winking.
He tested my latin, lent me Neitzsche and Hegel, but
        deprecated James Joyce.

My carpenter dad left me all his tools — useless to my
        hamfists
as pike and axe — dad's armoury, that hewed an ark for ten
        children.

Having no alternative, we choose a place — and learn to live.

And having learned – how, or why, choose somewhere else to
learn to die?

Upon a skyline graph of concrete blocks, a few, horned
Gothic towers
include a mock Florentine city hall, that Ruskin further
mocked;

and an old, stumpy cathedral, daily flying England's flag,
rallying
our crosspurposes of feet that hollow the stones of
Treadmill Street below.

Nearby, a granite Mr Forster's admonitory digit provokes
our local wits.
'Come winter ee'll be glad of a bit of warm birdshit on
that finger!'

West, on a heathered hill, climbs Haworth's chip-shop
crowded street,
haunted by inconsolable rain, and a mad parson's
improbable daughters.

Over cosy Coxwold, east, the wry review of stars, and the
long tooth
of the laughing moon, evoke an even more improbably
immortal Yorick.

And north, high meadows wrestle the encroaching fells –
our tiny toil
magnified in the heave and the haul of the great, sky-
shouldering dales.

Having no alternative, we choose a place – and learn to live.
And having learned – how, or why, choose somewhere else to
learn to die?

Averil King-Wilkinson

Winter Now at Biggin Hill

The blood-orange sun dies early
on the rim of a blue crater.
The abyss we lurch towards
is filled with wan stars,
and the dim ether of sleep.

In the tomb of winter,
decay ends, and becomes life.
A banshee vixen rents the vault,
a swan broods by the solid lake;
and amid the rimed branches,
the airmen wait with unquiet eyes.

They walk among the birches,
white limbs of dead dancers,
they are quilted against the iron frosts:
in their nostrils there is ice,
the trees have their tongues.

The runway leads to nowhere
past dark huts in the silent wood.
Their snow is shrapnel, their sun is blood:
yet we cannot kiss or laugh as they.
The ageless living watch the fleeting dead;
tonight is a long time ago.

Lotte Kramer

The Green God

Like spiders crouching in their nets
The men sit on the bank and fish
Inside their green umbrella-wheels,
Oblivious of the wind.

They come from valleys, from a sky
That bears the footnote of the hills,
From arteries of earth, they come,
That lead into the dark.

Now, bodies rooted to the grass,
They wait here, regularly spaced,
For the one heave that sucks and rings
The river's water course,

Disturbing patterns of the wind
Whose temper strikes into the glass
With long, uneven-hammered knives
That rush towards the sea.

We stand above them, watch them there,
Their Sunday worship of the Nene,
Their patient readiness to kill,
The Green God's homily.

Lotte Kramer

April Wind

Here, under the sky's wide wheel
The wind sharpens the day's blade.

April has come with abrupt
Harshness, mocking the shy sun,

Blazing the blossom's softness
Over the shivering grasses.

Shadows are as restless as
Nervous fingers, unable

To find the day's knot and measure;
Bullfinches, in a sudden fit,

Sit and strip our apple-tree
Of buds – so much destruction

Unrolling in this low land;
An augury of rough spring

Falling on hill country, one April,
Years ago, when the breaking

Of glass stunned my grandfather's
Heart, not dead, in this wind's cry.

Brenda Leckie

Sunbath

I'm the Old Man of the Sea
cat-napping on the beach
between shape-changes. Under my skin's
the skeleton of a bat, my feet
leave wolf-tracks in the sand, my hair
snakes in the breeze. The pebbles turn
beneath my belly as I stretch and yawn.
The sunlight pins me down,
and holds me to this form
for a moment only. Then
my bones erode. I'll become
a pillar of chalk, or a worm,
or a hawk, or a clod of earth. I gather
my atoms together, against
the destruction of the tide, lest I should change
untimely to a jellyfish, and sprawl
formless and insensate on the shore.

J. Longwill

My Father

'2309252 Sergeant James Longwill

Served overseas: France 7.10.15 to 13.6.19
Singapore 27.8.39 to 14.2.42
POW (Far East) 15.2.42 to 8.11.45
Discharged on ceasing to fulfil Army physical requirements.'

A few miles
below his hillside grave

ships. Iron
and sulphurous air.

There I think of him
and of others like him.

Between them and England,
as between me and him,
I say it in that Burmese word

Sokiebiami, the desired earth.

Bette McArdle

Christmas Mart

One December afternoon a hyacinth
grey and lemon sky leaned
on the black town hall clock
the tower railings of the sheriff court
the orange and yellow chimney pots.
I saw a woman waiting at a stop,
beside her on the ground a goose.
The woman was worn, dark, less
than perfect, but the goose was almost
manufactured looking till immaculately
it moved an eye. Then I met a man
with a duck over his arm
hanging by its strung and waxy feet.
Down the alley from the mart
came more – housewives and farmers,
butchers' boys – lights spread all over town;
everywhere I saw everyone accompanied
by some body of beatific creation,
feathered forms glowing in the cold
and deepening gloaming. I barely understood
my joy – the sheer headiness of
our eternal obligation to be
as beautiful as we can see,
as what we must consume.
The snowflakes melted on my singing tongue.
My soul-goose strung along with me
all through the darkest season
till after Hogmanay I told someone the love I felt;
You're drunk, she said. My goose became a dinner.
I would have done much better
to have left her flying free
than fatten her and tie her feet
and have her waddle round with me.

Bette McArdle

Rural School

Ackergill, Caithness, April Nineteen-O-Something

Pens stroke and scratch, dip in the china pots
that Phemie newly filled today; tight fingers
struggle, sweat, blot – the afternoon goes
slowly, drowsily, measured by sliding spots
of sunlight across the pleats of my new
pinafore, down my button boots, leaping over teacher's
dais and up the varnished wall. Effie's
tongue, I know, is sliding out
for all I only see the fair springs
caught in gold about her cheek.
The schoolroom clock tocks heavy in the silence
in the silence, on the wall, securing us
to the earthbeat of the world's heart
in our carbolic coffin, brass-handled.
Something very important is about to happen
or perhaps it is this moment, somehow
within time and us. Brilliant
beyond the window the road
runs all the way to Wick
or maybe further. It comes and goes and yet
is there. But not as green fields, patchwork
quilted, stay. The boys will take the road
to market, sea, to soldier, to be apprenticed
as watchmakers, coopers, masons, while we
marry and stitch the fields and fences in place.
Teacher, catching my eye,
frowns, checks his watch
linked by the albert
on his dark serge breast,
pushes the spectacles up his nose
and notes his log: 'April 10 – The windows should be
            widened;
it is good for children to look out
upon roads and green fields.'

Medbh McGuckian

The Butterfly Farm

The film of a butterfly ensures that it is dead:
Its silence like the green cocoon of the car-wash,
Its passion for water to uncloud.

In the Japanese tea-house they believe
In making the most of the bright nights,
That the front of a leaf is male, the back female.

There are grass stains on their white stockings;
In artificial sun even the sound are disposable;
The mosaic of their wings is spun from blood.

Cyanide in the killing-jar relaxes the Indian moon moth,
The pearl-bordered beauty, the clouded yellow,
The painted lady, the silver-washed blue.

Medbh McGuckian

Aunts

My aunts jived their way
Through the Fifties to my teens.
They lay till noon and called me up
To listen for their lovers at the gate,
And paid me for the colour of their eyes –
'Grey', I said, or 'Brown', when they wanted
Blue or hazel, in their giggling,
Sleeping-together dreams.

I watched them shading in their lips
From sugar pink to coral, from mulberry to rose,
And their wet skirts hungry for
The brilliance of their swing,
As they dried by the strange
Elastic girdles, paper petticoats.

Once out of the blue
I caught them dancing on the bed,
With their undergrowth of hazel,
And their make-up sweated through.

Jane McLaughlin

Cargo Cult

Ash of the moon burned them in the dawn
setting grey on cinder mountains
streaming the desert air they came
up roads niello silver before
the sun shook foil over the landscape.

Word had come that the icebox landed
massed as for prayer or music they stood
grey faces whispering a web
in the morning wind.
A white cuboid on a black rock
silent, milk-calm, above them.

By their will the door is opened:
the gifts move towards them. Frosted,
glistening with rime the earth-fruits,
lemon, guava, pepper, every
gourd and legume the land bears,
a rustling glacier
of frozen colours pouring endless
across the valley floor.

The sign is accepted: they
are satisfied.
Sun plates the ranges with light.

Scarabs metallic crimson and blue
strung to the horizon strike like matches
as the sun hits
and from each wells a flower
brighter and fiercer
than the molten cactus.

Mary Michaels

twilight

1

it's almost ten o'clock
        still light outside
we are in bed

except for the roses and bowl of fruit
right by the window
everything in the room is grey

he falls asleep

I begin to hear the sound of his breathing
a light
broken
singing
        sound

one moment it swells in the shrilling of birds
taking off from a tree outside

then it is thin
regular
quiet

later
the rattle and hiss of the leaves
takes it over again

later
it rains
and
he wakes

he makes the most
deep sighs
every five minutes or so

'what's the matter?'

'nothing
        – it just feels as if I'm living at a high altitude'

'what does that mean?'

'as if the air is very thin'

in the night I can hear him again

taking in air through his mouth
and pushing it out
from the top of his lungs

he is the child who
has jumped into the swimming pool
missed the expected footing
and over a long
long
minute
sees the horizon line of the water
fall and then rise
over his face
while he tries to push out
whatever it is
that is burning inside his chest

the moment of living-or-drowning
is stretched into months
for him

just getting light
too early
for even the birds

he seems to be sleeping

I work myself out of my bed
and make my way over
his mattress
the clothes on the floor
and the waste-paper basket
into the kitchen

the kitchen is down a step

I quietly close the door behind me
pick up the kettle
turn on the tap

the twilight seems spacious in here

the blue flame against the enamel
                                    surprising
where everything else is
subdued

Anthony Mortimer

Silas Watkin, 1830

Although this evening one could dream of prophets
Floating white beards upon the fluent air,
Or lithe young angels strolling through the orchard
With everlasting ripeness in their arms,
I do not think this land was ever Beulah.
The soil that grains my skin has come too close
For comfort in the promise of these fields,
Made to our measure, but not made for us.

Some hail the spark that flames the master's rick
As holy fire in a peasant's hand:
Others remember how the story says
A shepherd-lad will cut the giant down.
In God's good time, perhaps, not mine; my scythe
Swings slowly, and the heads of poppies fall.

Norman Nicholson

Shingle

It surges down –
Slow underpull
Of heavy grey waves,
Meeting the sea's
Surge upwards.

Never a backflow, always
This crawl of a fall.
On the line of the swell
Each long crest crumbles
Into a sud of stone
Medallions and ovals,
Smooth as butterbeans;
But the shoulder of the wave
Is cumbered with cobbles
The size a stone-waller
Might pile into a barn.

At the bank's bottom step
The obtuse-angled
Thrust of the tide
Shovels the pebbles
Inwards and slant-wise,
For the surf to suck back again
The breadth of a winkle-shell
From where they were before.

A mounded migration
Of crab-backed stones,
Tide by tide, moves
Sideways along the shore.

But here at the highest
Rung of the rise –

A gull's stride under
The shivering overhang
Of sea-spurge and marram –
Only the wildest
Tides arrive
To dump sacks of boulders
On the shrivelled wrack,
Where the stones reside
A while on their circuit,
Inch by inch
Rolling round England.

Norman Nicholson

On the Dismantling of Millom Ironworks

'Child of the clouds! remote from every taint
Of sordid industry thy lot is cast.'
William Wordsworth, *The River Duddon*, Sonnet 2.

I laughed once at those words – for there, near where he
    pondered
On Duddon Bridge, shallow-draft barges shot their ore,
Even in Wordsworth's day, for the charcoal-burning
    furnace
Sited like a badger's set deep in Duddon woods.
Twenty years on, at the river's mouth, the Hodbarrow
    miners
Kicked up mountainous molehills; a conifer copse of
    chimneys
Criss-crossed the west with spikes and laterals, and
    landslides of limestone
Walled off all sight of the tide. The river seeped from the
    marshes
In a flux of haematite. Today, two life-times later,
Bled white of every stain of ore, the Duddon rediscovers
Its former channel almost unencumbered – mines
Drowned under stagnant waters, chimneys felled and
    uprooted,
Slagbanks ploughed down to half their height, all
    cragginess,
Scrag-end and scree ironed out, and re-soiled and greened
    over
To long sulky drumlins, dumped there by the look of
    them
An ice-age ago. They cut up the carcass of the old
    ironworks
Like a fat beast in a slaughter-house; they shovelled my
    childhood
On to a rubbish heap. Here my father's father,

Foreman of the back furnace, un-sluiced the metal lava
To slop in fiery gutters across the foundry floor
And boil round the workmen's boots; here five generations
Toasted the bread they earned at a thousand degrees
                    Fahrenheit
And the town thrived on its iron diet. On the same
                    ground now,
Split foundations moulder in the sea air; blizzards
Of slag-grey dust are blown through broken Main Gate
                    uprights;
Reservoir tanks gape dry beside cracked, empty pig-beds;
And one last core of clinker, like the stump of a dead
                    volcano,
Juts up jagged and unblastable. – Stand on the ricketty
                    pier,
Look left along the line where gantry and crane and coke-
                    bank
Ten years ago blocked all the view – and now you're
                    staring
Bang at Black Combe. The wind resumes its Right of
                    Way;
Shelduck fly low from feeding-ground to feeding-ground,
No intervening chimneys forcing an upward flight.
In parallel troughs once dug for the long-since-rotted
                    sleepers
That carried the rails to the tip, cardboard and tags of
                    sacking
Accumulate mulch for docks and the shunting-yards
                    succumb
To a yellow encroachment of ragwort. The town shrinks
                    and dwindles.
Old People's Bungalows creak half-way up the hill,
Over a mile away, and privet hedge and hydrangea
Screen out even the memory of smoke and slag. An age
Is pensioned off – its hopes, gains, profits, desperations
Put into mothballs. A hundred years of the Bessemer
                    process –
The proud battery of chimneys, the hell-mouth roar of the
                    furnace,
The midnight sunsets ladled across a cloudy sky –
Are archeological data, and the great-great-great-

grandchildren
Of my grandfather's one-time workmates now scrounge
        this iron track
For tors and alleys of ore bunkered in the cinders and the
        hogweed.
And maybe the ghost of Wordsworth, seeing further than I
        can,
Will stare from Duddon Bridge, along miles of sand and
        mud-flats,
To a peninsula bare as it used to be, and, beyond, to a
        river,
Back in its old course, aimed square at the open sea,
Flowing, untainted now, to a bleak, depopulated shore.

Dennis O'Driscoll

Meat

1

Like plums
we ripen
on stiff kernel:

a classical interior;
carved bust of skull,
smooth pillars of limb.

2

A hot kebab
at body heat,
rotting, going off.

Meat on the bone.
No freezer deep enough
to keep it fresh.

3

A double heart transplant:
your heart and mine
beating in time.

Buried in a single body, live,
two lovers
lying in one bed.

4

I look at books,
anatomy charts.
I kiss you,

muscle, tissue, heart.
Your soft flesh cushions me
from the reality of bone.

Maggie O'Sullivan

here now

1

I walk to the edge of the beach.
A man swings
distant above the sea.
Stripes curve to the balloon
grey and green.
Above his body blue runs.
Turning,
I lower myself, inch by inch,
to the sea.

2

No seagulls
no jagged waves

heat replaces cold

I am here now

Here everything
that I walk through
is as clear as you promised

the sand
easing
into my footprints.

3

Cocks roughen the night,
then other species of birds,
one after another,
dismantle the dawn.

The ringing bell of the church
and workmen
with hammers and saws
erect the morning.

4

The door is open in the single storey building.
From grey-green foliage
geraniums wander
toward me.

In this pure light
stone has the lustre of marble,
green shuttered windows
have the boldness of endurance.

Clematis and sunflowers
pile one on another,
commit themselves
to a feudal community.

Rodney Pybus

Papyrus in a Sydney Library

A few words scraped from history –
the wrapping, fragile as dead skin,
from some Egyptian corpse or other
carries a bare dozen lines of Greek,
gap-toothed with age or moths.
But enough to set off the old rhythms
as I read, despite my stuttering recall.

I let my eyes close the better to catch
the sway, the keen pulse of the chant,
to re-test the imprint of rosy-fingered dawn,
crafty Odysseus, and the wine-dark sea.
But the years have slipped in
too many lacunae. I sift in vain
and look at a scholar's notes,
and back again to the text:
each letter precise, as discretely formed
as the elegant patterning of the saga,
the words run together as if in Greek
there were no need to pause,
the lines so magical
they might pace themselves.

Yet here the wanderer's drifted too far south,
pinned and staked under library glass,
in a vast island where only the sunlight
scorching off the sand, and the sea
as dark as burgundy or the Hellespont
are bewitchingly familiar;
but the gods are alien,
and the lotus-eaters displaced and anxious.

Mere 'nostalgia' gets it wrong.
It's the yawning pain of home-sickness

like concentrated famine
that's so carefully expressed
into these syllables torn from the north.

Rodney Pybus

Knapping

I sat long, working out of the flint
a memory. Practising, in my fashion.
Tap, tap, tap. Splinters leapt off,

painfully: I was not striking
quite at the right angle – the brittle
mottled spikes pricked and stung

like sparks my still clumsy hand.
Nearly. Nearly there.
I stared inwards: the first light

seeping over a loch. Bleeding a little.
Water like ice out of season,
smoother in fact than my flint:

tap, tap, tap. That edge again,
that precision – brighter now,
the sun slowly lifting the hill-top

up into the night-washed air.
Still specks of lint on the blue.
A last tap at the flint, and I've worked

out of it the memory, now so
honed that I shall not feel
but see myself not resisting

but separating, opening to it;
the light streaming into the lake
cuts shadows out of itself

along branches, behind stones,
with more speed and grace than I
working time out of another flint.

P. F. Ritchie

Of Burke and Wills
and the Third Man

When William John Wills cut the poor nag's throat
And cupped his hands to catch the blood
Robert O'Hara Burke believed for a time
That the surveyor had slain the sun.
But on reading his leader's thought
The third man mocked him in his stride
By pointing to the fireball in the sky.
'A pity, Mr Burke,' he said,
'That you didn't catch it on the rise.'
Burke, who couldn't spit wet just then
Released the mottled gibber from his mouth.
'Mr King,' he croaked, 'you are free to go your own way
          now
Or if you want . . . follow at your will.'
'I follow nothing but the sun,' King said,
And pointed to a pile of crimson bowels.
Taking his knife, Burke struck the man shadow on the
          ground
A desperate act which drove King to take cover.
Later, when the knowledge of his isolation
Grew to disproportionate size
He took it upon himself to stumble east
When a saner man would have stumbled south.
That same night at firelight Burke and Wills joined hands
While King, bruised and shaken by his falls
Crawled into an unknown creature's grave
To escape the light.
On the tide of morning, however,
He took the precaution to guard his shadow on the ground
As the leader, ape-miming up a tree
Cursed the distant beast cavorting on all fours.

Only Wills was wise.
He saved his mime for the next day's rasper
And ever so quietly died.

Peter Robinson

Dirty Language

He would sit impassive at the window;
lodged behind the cream cloth covers
of somebody or other's Collected Works,
    would appear unmoved.

His time is dirt. Unrinsed empties
fill work surfaces, the tear-off calendar
    a week or so too thick.

It isn't you that worries me; it's what
    you do to things.

If he would wash his thinning haircut
in the basin, no, once there he'll only
    watch himself grow old.

And it falls to me to disentangle
hairs from the sink plug, stuck
to my soap so firmly you would think
    he hoarded them.

In the cabinet mirror, I see decay
proliferates from the face. Beneath it,
    silver paper wrinkles.

Collecting dust like dirty language, crumbs,
the mug rings, toilet wall inscriptions:
    the so and so was here.

Now it reaches everywhere. The days
trickle onto lino like a waterfall.
Sun sets for him at the window,
    when I close the curtains.

By artificial light, the darkness, this
  swells out of all proportion.

I polish the kettle, tarnished as
the word he uses, until my distorted
  features show through.

It makes no difference what I say.

Carol Rumens

In Pear Tree Road

Only plane trees stood
now, in Pear Tree Road.
My father mourned white orchards,
but I was glad,

especially in Autumn
when the wind lay tiles
of their broad, delicate leaves
to colour the stone miles.

I kicked them high and wide;
pleased with the patterns, took
a rustling quire of them
to page my heaviest book.

Many were merely brown,
some still green as May:
the best had put on all
their rich seasons to die,

hanging tight until
that final crimsoning
when the small sun had pressed
a flame hand to each skin.

Lawrence Sail

Eating Maize

From the very first, it has been
a history of destructions:
the long leaves wincing,
silky tassels torn away
from buttery knuckles clenched
as tightly as a grenade.

Year after year I suck
the sweet and yellowed bone
of rich summer, teeth
burrowing inwards until
the racks are hollow, and I hold
nothing but tough litter.

Then I dream how with one
long and careful cut
I might find, inside the core
a whole hillside crackling
with head-high plantations,
acres of solid fruit.

Supreme illusionist,
I can recreate hope
endlessly, like a set
of gleaming Russian dolls
by caesarean section
out of a single season.

Yet from the first, it was
a history of destructions:
in winter I see myself
as an old but never replete
cannibal eating my heart out
with a terrible hunger for innocence.

Valerie Sinason

Coffee Break

The Lebanese woman offers me
sweet-smelling coffee.
She dined at Maxim's last week.
Last month Beirut –
next month Saudi.

Her friend,
the East European aristocrat,
bedsits in Hiltons.
'It is so convenient.
They have them everywhere.'

My child plays in her vast carpeted halls,
rides Arab rocking horses,
drops Action Man on a jewelled cushion.

Outside
it is still London.

The aristocrat won't return to Russia.
They seized her palace during the revolution.
Her family left in a friend's yacht.

My grandfather left Russia in the hold of a ship.
Escaped from pogroms to work in a Welsh mine.

Even our points of contact divide us.

The maid hovers.
She was flown in from Africa last week.
'The Europeans don't know how to serve.
But this one had never seen a fridge
or a hoover!'

The maid is worrying about the famine
in her country.
Their laughter stabs at her
like tiny cocktail sticks,
buries her words under jellied fruits.

They talk of oil.
Pipelines cross central heating.
Sheik Yemani is so handsome,
a credit to his family . . .

I become microscopic,
a Western insect on a carved fruitbowl.

The maid hovers.
My child dances in the hall.

Outside
it is still London.

A. H. Snow

How We Took the Bad News

At last Davis got through to us.
We presumed it was Davis.
He was half an hour late.
Then came the familiar crackle
and we knew he was on the air.
The screen went blue. A white
square appeared in the centre.
It remained there motionless.
This puzzled us. We were waiting
for his usual grin, his diagrams
and long-distance shots that showed
a touch of genius. I heard Jeffes
draw in his breath. 'Why
doesn't he speak?' Moira sat
with her pencil ready. His reports
had always been brief, lucid and above all, exciting.
Then we heard his voice. It was him,
there was no doubt about it. Not words. Just flat
squares of sound repeated
at precise mathematical intervals.
Suddenly the screen went red.
A white triangle this time.
Equilateral. Right in the centre.
Then came the voice. It was jerking
out sharp triangles of sound
in a steady mechanical rhythm.
Something fell on the table before me.
It was a convex blob of sweat.
Now the screen was yellow.
A white circle occupied the exact centre.
Davis's voice was booming like a church bell.
It stopped. The colour left the screen.
We saw everything again in black and white,
the square, the triangle, the circle.

Then they were all together, super-imposed
on the same axis, as if skewered
on an invisible pin. The square
which was at the back, began to revolve
clockwise. The triangle, anti-clockwise.
You couldn't tell if the circle was revolving.
The speed of revolutions increased.
The image slowly faded, leaving the screen
black, silent.
I looked round. Jeffes had collapsed
with his head and arms on the table.
Ashmour was still staring.
Moira was sobbing in silence.
'They've won,' she murmured.
We knew then that nothing
would save us. Not even suicide.

John Stathatos

In Passage

1

'Our observed latitude was south of the Equator
31 degrees 37 minutes, the longitude 334 degrees
51 minutes, the mean course south-south-west, the
wind south, south by east, south-south-west and
south-west, lower sail's, topsail's and top-gallant
sail's breeze, unstable weather with a thick sky.'

2

Thick sky, the air
thicker yet.
Week after listless week
the city lies in a heat wave,
caught by sargasso
    drifted to strange latitudes.
Days flat and monochrome: rainless,
yet damp seeps steadily out of grey stone
to hang above the rooftops.
The compass rose reduced to ornament.

3

The townscape insubstantial,
will-o'-the-wisp, still air,
coming alive only at dusk,
at nightfall. Endless evenings,
a light increasingly unreal
as it slips into dark.
We wait upon the change.
Across the elevated motorway
tower blocks loom against the sky,
glimmer with portholes,
tug at anchor

ready to cast off.

4

How to speak of the light?
Tonight, a wash of lilac in the east
darkens to gentian and ultramarine.
Dark floods up from the streets,
laps at windows, breaks over roofs;
the sky above
luminous
for long minutes still.

5

Hemmed in by trees, my street
creaks and changes.
As the city grows emptier
great trees move in,
taking over block after block.
The northern suburbs rustle to themselves.
On Hampstead Hill
the light
        darker
               beneath the trees.

6

Walking these streets
one needs no bearings,
a scrap of Mozart is enough
snatched from a lighted window:
'Osservate, leggete con me . . .'
winding among the poplars.
This is no season for decisions.

7

The waterways lead to the sea,
estuaries and tidal flats
where wire rusts slowly down into the mud.
New moon
etched above the canals:

135

touch gold.
A sense of emptiness by dawn.
Days tread upon each other's heels,
while Jacob Roggeveen sails on
lost on the wide Pacific.

At last the rains.

8

'The estimated southern latitude 15 degrees 8 minutes,
and the longitude 228 degrees 23 minutes, the course
20 miles, the wind very variable, thus calm, north-east,
north, west, again north and north-east, top-gallantsail's
also topsail's breeze, stormy weather with rain. Saw
                    weeds,
mews, and among these a black bird with a wide breast,
which was unknown to many and by others was held to
                    be a
watersnipe or like kind, giving a flute-like sound.'

Alaric Sumner

Portrait Two

She says: 'I soak my feet in hot water
to soften my toe-nails, because otherwise
they are too hard to cut, and with my weak wrists
I can't do anything too strenuous, though I used to
ride a bicycle, and I used to walk round Bedfordshire,
but there are no large hills, well, except for
        Moggerhanger,
and that other one up to the north, and help Dad in the
        allotment;
and then he just cycled past and said, "Ot, ini?", and
I took years to understand those strange accents, well,
I was Kentish born and daughter to a school master
and the cold is worse though the heat does
bring on my dizzy spells and I can't
have my head in the sun, not in direct sunlight,
and she fainted and there I was all
done up in this plaster hood (I had TB in the neck
you know, and I wasn't allowed to move my head at all),
and anyway, there I was with this plaster and there she
        was
all fainted on the floor and he says,
"I'm just off round the shops then," well, would
you credit it? "I'm just off. . . .", that's all,
"I'm just off. . . .", for cigarettes, disgusting habit,
and that dog got that hare all by mistake,
there he was and he was so stupid (the dog, I mean),
he'd just given up and was going off to do something else,
when the poor hare doubled back and almost
hit him and the great big thing and he
tried to drag it, looking at me all sad,
and I said, "Oh no!" I said, "Oh no!
You caught the blessed thing, you caught it,
now you can carry it home," I said, but he
buried it and the stink when he brought

137

rabbits and things and all the times
I had to clear up after he had
been dirty, he got incontinent when he was
getting old, Dad did, and anyway he never used
enough toilet paper (too mean) and in the end I just
couldn't go on, I felt terrible, but what with
him seeing his "wireless bugs" all over,
yes, little wirelesses with legs (perhaps
they listened too, like Watergate, you know,
or perhaps just the insects) and the doctors
had to cope then and I was all on my own
and I hadn't enjoyed myself more since
being a little girl in the Bishop's Palace and all
the books I read. *Anna Karenina. War and Peace.*
Books. And walks; by the beach; in the moonlight.
Yes. And I think I'll go to bed directly. Yes.
Yes, I was happy then. They had quite a good selection.
All things considered. *War and Peace. Emma.* Nothing too
        modern.'
And she leans back in her chair with her eyes closed,
her lips pursed and her hands clasped in her lap.

James Sutherland-Smith

An Exhibition of Musical Instruments: Victoria and Albert Museum

A love of detail makes a world
Of fretwork or moral pictures
Varnished above clavier strings.
Such boudoir sensibility
Thickens to textures of moth flight,
Weights moth rest with importances
Of seconds, dusting leaves with talc.
It requires nothing more or less
Than regular music playing
Behind lampblack wrought-iron gates;
Murmuring above displays of
English eighteenth-century dress.

Tromba marina, theorbo,
Claviorganum, epinette,
Bell harp, cittern, hurdy-gurdy,
Crwth, quinton, viola d'amore,
Pitch pipe, bird pipe, vox humana;
Linnean instruments denote
A copse composed of touch and breath
Where hems are lifted and darkness
Creaks with rational argument
Or is enlightened by ruffled
English eighteenth-century dress.

The poisoned silk weaver, smallpox,
Grave robbers, a resistance to
Enclosure, mutiny, scurvy,
Gin, syphilis, the filthy Thames
Are discords from a lack of wit.
In the arbor of well temper
Watch the woodpecker stuck to bark
Ornament of health while madness

Of wind and rain muddies others'
English eighteenth-century dress.

From here we can see a balance
Of nature and cultivation.
Panic is a grace note – ivy
Round a folly. Much fear, much more
Fear requires heavy instruments;
The percussive wilderness struck
With axes. Exchange or dispute
With me fingering strawberries
To plucked sweetness which means as much
As love to you, once bitterness
So much that you can never let
Unmeasured intervals distress
English eighteenth-century dress.

James Sutherland-Smith

The Maiden in the Wood

The wood was always imaginary.
But she can know this and still enter
Where the moss bank glows like billiard felt
And the mannerly leaves hang like linen.

She always walks there with her father
To that perfect meadow undulating
Above watercress ditches, a network
Of filtered water and sterile gravel.

She always thinks of this with lovers.
The thought is easy as a change of tense.
Hands settling round her hips like cotton,
Lips tickling her hair like lace are always

Will be or was. She is never
Darkened by owl purpose or fox stink
As she lies and dreams of dancing
In the wood's taut unaltered radiance.

For this new man tenderness showers
On the wood. Girlishly his nipples itch
While she kisses them. But, when sensations
From his touch flow in her, she sinks back

So it seems as if as many years
Ago as childhood that she said
'I've never been able to cry.'
And now he moans to what he might

Later call a first maturity.
He slides upon her smoothly as a quilt.
He's unprepared for the sudden boredom.
She was so close and is so close to tears.

George Szirtes

Education

1

This woman is teaching her child the sense of touch.
'Look here. Touch the air now. Is it damp?' He feels
her warm hands on his wrist. 'Concentrate,' she says,
'Feel the air before you, how it gives way.'
He feels the folds of her cloth on his legs.
'Prod it, move it. It's clean, everywhere.' The throne
          grows
up around them. They must sit down. There must
always be rest after education.

2

See here – life is a voyage –
I must set my star in the ceiling
and be off across the city of fish
where the bells are silent and masts are bones
and all prows echo my own features.
I adjust my loincloth and feel the rough slap
of hessian on my chest. The air is rare
and is getting colder. One must
acquit oneself etcetera, so cheerybye –
my star draws me like a magnet and
I am rigid as iron. This damn thing is leaky
but in order to get to one's destination
one must get one's feet wet.

3

There is always the question, Why?
Even when the answer is perfectly obvious. Why?
says the glance toward heaven
in spite of its investments there. Why?
the craned necks of examination.

Why? the inviting armchair.

The walls are marble, streaked and veined
in marvellous colours from which
heads project. These accept
and never ask the obvious questions.

And the old man lying there
seems happy enough to see the bothersome syllable
disintegrate into mere cleanliness.

Isobel Thrilling

The Miner

The old miner grew
gooseberries;
gold and green
and bursting with sunlight.

He trained
unlikely butterflies
of sweet-pea,
his allotment was an oasis
of cabbages and beans.

At home
his helmet stood in its
usual place.
It had held his thoughts,
protected his vision
of sky and soil,
when he fought the darkness.

He still touched it
with respect;
a piece of rare armour.

John Wakeman

A Sea Family

A still-born boy is wrapped
in clean matting
and the Niger takes him gently
to the sea and an old drunk
kicked to death in Glasgow his broken face
veined like the map of Skye where he was born
makes his way out through the Firth of Clyde
submerged to avoid interfering policemen
and out and out and out sneaking past Ireland
to the sea which was always in his alcoholic blood
though forgotten except in good dreams
and a girl in a village near Lisbon
passes the white sailors' church
forgetting the fat postman who took her
once to the cinema and never dared again
so she steps at dawn into the pearly sea
believing that no one has ever loved her
and the old man hugs the baby
to his smashed ribs and the girl
holds them safe in her flayed arms
and they converse together
and stroll with the tides and the turning moon
amazed at the bright ships and the great fishes.

John Wakeman

Love in Brooklyn

'I love you, Horowitz,' he said, and blew his nose.
She splashed her drink. 'The hell you say,' she said.
Then, thinking hard, she lit a cigarette:
'Not *love*. You don't *love* me. You like my legs,
and how I make your letters nice and all.
You drunk your drink too fast. You don't love *me*.'

'You wanna bet?' he asked. 'You wanna bet?
I loved you since the day they moved you up
from Payroll, last July. I watched you, right?
You sat there on that typing chair you have
and swung round like a kid. It made me shake.
Like once, in World War II, I saw a tank
slide through some trees at dawn like it was god.
That's how you make me feel. I don't know why.'

She turned towards him, then sat back and grinned,
and on the bar stool swung full circle round.
'You think I'm like a tank, you mean?' she asked.
'Some fellers tell me nicer things than that.'
But then she saw his face and touched his arm
and softly said 'I'm only kidding you.'

He ordered drinks, the same again, and paid:
a fat man, wordless, staring at the floor.
She took his hand in hers and pressed it hard
and his plump fingers trembled in her lap.

Jack Winter

The tax collector

Riding through
rural Ruritania
collecting air tax
for the Mogul
I was signalled
from the roadside
by a dragon.

It was her scales
I was not prepared for.

Red they were
and glistening
like blood
on a shilling
remarkable really
like thumb prints
on a ledger
and in any case
I stopped.

Kiss me
she said.

They really were
the most remarkable scales
like oil drops on an apple
like tears in consommé.

When I did
what she had asked
kissed her that is
and she was blond again
and creamy thighed

I did not know
how to tell her
it was the dragon
that I loved.

My mother's stitchery . . .

My mother's stitchery
by oil-light, bright needle
pricking linen with petals
taut as a tambourine
beneath tight black eyes

Come quick, my father calls
come do something useful.
She anchors the skein
who never did anything
not useful, but this

They kneel down together
in the sty by oil-light
the feverish sow between them
a small sister, brown hands
travelling her white lard

Your mother was beautiful
father tells me one day.
It is a strange saying.
His eyes that have seen more
than mine seem to see less

That fine work by oil-light
he tells her, wrinkles your eyes
but occasions for it
don't stop, nor she, save to suck
new silk for the needle's eye

All her care is dispersed
now, given or gone away
under some several roofs
my sisters and I
all her useless stitchery

When the air though cold . . .

When the air though cold
hung heavily in the trees
I heard a pig's scream
and looked out – an arena
at the forest's edge
where a desperate dog-wolf
chased one of our young

A piglet runs like a cat
ears flat, stops so fast
with all its trotters dug in
grinning in its fear
that the grey beast overruns
and snarling turns back
on the pale scampering thing

Then it seems success
turns the pig's head from terror
to playfulness till
its squealing is with laughter
and the dog-wolf too
relaxes despite hunger
fangs sure then of lard

Whether or not I dreamt this
or saw in the flesh
circus at the forest's edge
when the air though cold
hung heavily in the trees
I heard the pig's scream
bubble softly and turn red

Notes on the Poets

Gillian Allnutt was born in 1949 and lives in London. She regards herself as a professional writer but also teaches in Further and Adult Education. Poems have been published in *Bananas, Gallery, Limestone, Spare Rib:* she has published short stories in *Time Out* and *Spare Rib.* She won the Stroud Festival International Poetry Competition in 1978.

Joan Barton was born in Bristol in 1908 and has been a bookseller for the last thirty-two years. A collection of her poems, *The Mistress,* appeared in 1972, and a second, *Ten Poems,* was published in a limited edition in 1979. She was awarded a Southern Arts Association Literature Bursary in 1978.

Jane Beeson has published poetry during the past three years in magazines including *New Poetry, Poetry Review* and others. She has also broadcast her poetry on two occasions in the BBC's series *Poetry Now.* Her plays have been broadcast. She lives and works in Devon. Her poem was first published in the magazine *New Poetry.*

James Berry was born in a Jamaican village, which he still visits. He has lived in London for twenty-five years. A selection of his poems, *Lucy's Letter,* was published in 1975 and another, *Fractured Circles,* in 1979. He has edited an anthology of twelve Caribbean poets, *Bluefoot Traveller.* He is involved in multi-ethnic education. In 1977/78 he was awarded a C. Day Lewis Fellowship at Vauxhall Manor Comprehensive School, London.

Peter Bland is a Yorkshireman who spent many years in New Zealand where he published four collections of poetry and a number of plays. He now lives in London working as a freelance writer and actor. *Mr Maui,* his first English collection of poetry, was published in 1976 by London Magazine Editions, and was a Poetry Book Society Recommendation. He recently received a Cholmondeley Award.

Cecily Deirdre Bomberg was born in London of an Irish Catholic mother and a Jewish father. She was educated at convent boarding schools in England and Eire. Her poems have appeared in *Adam International Review, The Antigonish Review, The Freethinker* etc., and in *New Poetry 3.*

Stewart Brown was born in 1951 in Southampton. His poems have been published in various magazines and anthologies in the UK, the USA and in the Caribbean where he taught for some time. Three collections of his poems have been published and he has received a Gregory Award (1975) and a South West Arts Literature Award (1978).

Alan Brownjohn's most recent volumes of poetry are *Warrior's Career* and *A Song of Good Life.* He was poetry critic of the *New Statesman* for seven years and, more recently, of *Encounter.* He has written a monograph on Philip Larkin in the British Council *Writers and their Work* series. He received a Cholmondeley Award for Poetry in 1979.

Carol Bruggen was born in Blackburn, Lancashire, in 1932. She was educated at Wycombe Abbey, University College of the South West and St Katharine's College, Liverpool. Her poems have been published by the Mid-Pennine Association, Quill Books, in the PEN Anthology (1977–78) and in little magazines. She has read her poems for local radio and her play, *The Albums,* was broadcast in 1977.

Tom Callaghan was born in 1955 in Sunderland. He grew up in Rochdale and was educated at Vassar College, New York, and at York where he now lives. He is working on a long series of poems, *Bone.*

Bruton Connors is the pen-name of Edward Rohen, who was born in 1931 in Dowlais, South Wales, and educated at Cardiff College of Art. He served with the army in Korea, taught in British Columbia and travelled in Mexico and the USA. He has contributed poetry and fiction to *Twentieth Century, Poetry Wales,* Arts Council anthologies and other publications. *Nightpriest,* a collection of poems, was published in 1965.

David Constantine was born in 1944 in Salford, Lancashire; he was educated at Manchester Grammar School and the University of Oxford. He lectures in German at the University of Durham. His poems have appeared in *New Poetry, The Cornish Review* and other magazines: his prose and poetry have appeared in *Stand*. He has a part in an anthology of North-Eastern poets, to be published this autumn, and a volume of his own next spring, both in Bloodaxe Books.

Neil Corcoran teaches English literature at Sheffield University. He has published various articles and reviews, mainly on modern poetry.

Iain Crichton Smith was born on the island of Lewis in 1928. He writes in English and Gaelic. He has written poems in both languages, as well as novels, and short stories. *An End to Autumn* (Gollancz) and *An T.-Aonaran* (in Gaelic), are novels, and his latest poetry book is *In the Middle* (Gollancz).

Hilary Davies was born in London in 1954 of Anglo-Welsh parents, and is a graduate student at Wadham College, Oxford. She edits *Argo,* a new literary magazine published in Oxford and Yale, and she has translated for Phaidon Press. Her poetry has been published in *The Bark and the Bite.*

Jessica d'Este lives in London and her poems have appeared in *New Poetry, Tribune, Jewish Chronicle* and in other magazines. Her poems have also been broadcast in the BBC programme, *Poetry Now.*

Patric Dickinson was born in 1914 and educated at St Catharine's College, Cambridge. His publications include *Selected Poems, A Wintering Tree, The Bearing Beast* and his autobiography *The Good Minute.* He has translated Vergil: *The Aeneid;* and *Aristophanes: The Complete Plays.* A new collection, *Our Living John,* is to be published this autumn.

Mary Dougherty (Bartlett) was born in 1949 in Eau Claire, Wisconsin. She won the Ina Coolebrith Prize for 1978, and has published in a number of journals and magazines. She is currently living in the South of France with her husband and two children.

Joan Downar was born in London and teaches in Nottingham. Her poems have been published in various magazines. *River People* (1976) was published by the Mandeville Press.

Stephen Duncan was born in London where he lives and works as a sculptor. He studied at Wimbledon School of Art and The Royal Academy of Art (1970–77). He teaches part-time at The Adelaide Centre for Kingsway CFE. He has published poems in *The Critical Review* and *Matrix*.

Jean Earle is English and has lived in different parts of Wales. She has published short stories, articles and 'in later middle life has turned completely to poetry'.

Harold Elvin is an artist on glass and steel, and has exhibited in Japan, Barbados, Norway and England. He has held a Winston Churchill Fellowship and travelled in Siberia, Mongolia and the Himalayas. He received an Arts Council grant for the continuation of his quartet, *A Gentle Russian*. For his book, *A Cockney in Moscow,* he received the Atlantic Award in Literature. He has published ten books: three are about his bicycle rides through the Orient and the Arctic.

Ricky Emanuel was born in Gravesend, Kent, studied at the University of Leeds, teaches English from time to time and lives and writes in the North Yorkshire Pennines.

Gavin Ewart was born in 1916. His most recent books of verse are *No Fool Like an Old Fool, Or Where a Young Penguin Lies Screaming,* both published by Gollancz, and *All My Little Ones* (Anvil Press Poetry). His *Collected Poems 1933–1980* will be published by Hutchinson in 1980.

Ruth Fainlight has published several collections of poetry including *The Region's Violence* and *Another Full Moon.* Her new book *Sibyls and Others,* will be published by Hutchinson in 1980.

Martyn A. Ford was born in Sutton Coldfield in 1949. He studied English and Art History at the University of Leeds, and has worked as a postman, civil servant and teacher of English. Since 1971 he has published poems, short stories and articles in a variety of magazines and newspapers. He received the Gregory Award (1978) and a short story prize from South East Arts. His poems appear in *Poetry South East*.

Robin Fulton was born in Scotland in 1937 and now lives in Scandinavia. Collections of his poetry include *Tree-Lines* (New Rivers Press, New York 1974), *Contemporary Scottish Poetry: Individuals and Contexts* (Macdonald, Edinburgh 1974) and *Between Flights* (Interim Press, Surrey 1977). He edited the quarterly *Lines Review* between 1967 and 1976 and has published six books of Swedish poetry in English. He held the Writer's Fellowship at Edinburgh University from 1969 to 1971.

Roger Garfitt edits *Poetry Review* and is currently Writer in Residence at Sunderland Polytechnic. In 1974 he received the Gregory Award for *West of Elm* published by Carcanet in 1975. His new collection *Unwritten Histories* will be published by Carcanet in 1980.

Jon Glover was born in 1943. He is married, with two daughters, and teaches at Bolton Institute of Technology. He has contributed in various ways to *Stand* since 1964, is joint editor, with Jon Silkin and Jeffrey Wainwright, of the Northern House Poetry series, and his poems and criticism have appeared in *Stand, Poetry Nation,* and *Poetry Review*. The poems in this anthology have appeared in *Stand* and on *Poetry Now* (BBC Radio 3).

W. S. Graham was born in Greenock, Scotland, in 1918 and became an engineer. In 1947 he received an Atlantic Award for Literature and lectured at New York University until 1948. He has read his poems on radio, television and in readings in the UK, US and Canada. His seven volumes of poetry are *The Seven Journeys* (William McLellan, Glasgow 1944), *Cage Without Grievance* (Parton Press 1942), *Second Poems* (Poetry London 1945), *The White Threshold* (Faber and Faber Ltd 1949), *The Nightfishing* (Faber 1955), *Implements in their Places* (Faber 1977), *Malcolm Mooney's Land* (Faber 1970). His *Collected Poems* is to be published by Faber in November 1979.

Teresa L. Gray was born in Birmingham in 1912 of Scots-Irish descent. She has written poetry since leaving school at fourteen years of age. She has worked in an office. Her poems have appeared in *Country Life,* the *Countryman* and other magazines.

Frederick Grubb was born in the 1930s. He has published poems, and a critical book, later essays on Philip Larkin, Edgell Rickword and others, and has edited a selection of poems and prose by Michael Roberts (Carcanet 1980).

Chris Hardy was born in 1947 in Nottingham and brought up in Africa and Malaysia as well as England. He was educated at the Universities of Kent and of London, and is now a guitarist and teacher. His poems have been published in various English magazines.

June Ella Harris was educated at a convent school. Her poems have appeared in small presses and in magazines.

Tony Harrison's poetry publications include *The Loiners* (1970), *Palladas: Poems* (1973) and *from The School of Eloquence & other poems* (1978). He has published for the theatre *Aikin Mata* (1964), *The Misanthrope* (1973), *Phaedra Britannica* (1975), *The Passion* (1977), *Bow Down* (1977) and a new libretto for Smetana's *Prodana Nevesta* (1978). He is at present living in New York.

Nora Holding was born and educated in Birmingham and now lives in Thanet, Kent. Her poetry has been published in various magazines including the *Countryman, Tribune, Poetry South East 2, 3* and *4,* and *New Poetry 4.*

Frances Horovitz was born in London in 1938 and educated at the University of Bristol and the Royal Academy of Dramatic Art. She is a poetry reader for BBC Radio 3 and 4 and the Open University and gives many live presentations of her own and other's work. Her publications include *The High Tower* (New Departures) and *Water Over Stone* (Enitharmon 1979).

Roger Howard taught at Peking University in 1972–74 and was an Arts Council Creative Writing Fellow at the University of York in 1976–78. In 1979 he was appointed Henfield Writing Fellow at the University of East Anglia. His poems have appeared in *New Poetry, Stand* and *The Times Literary Supplement.* His critical and theoretical writings have appeared in *Theatre Quarterly* and many other journals. He has published a biography, *Mao Tse-Tung and the Chinese People,* and has written over seventy plays.

Michael Hoyland has had poems published in the *Listener,* the *Scotsman* and other periodicals. He has broadcast about short stories and poetry, and writes about art.

Paul Hyland was born in Dorset in 1947. His poetry has been widely published and broadcast. In 1978 he published *Purbeck: The Ingrained Island* (Gollancz), *Riddles for Jack* (Northern House Poets) and *Domingus* (Mid-Day Publications). He received a Gregory Award for Poetry in 1976, and an Arts Council Writers Grant in 1979.

Trevor Innes was born in Lowestoft in 1946 and studied at the Universities of Oxford and Sheffield. He is now Head of English at Wheelwright Sixth Form College, Dewsbury. His poems have appeared in magazines and anthologies and have been broadcast.

Jenny Joseph was born in Birmingham and has spent most of her life in Southern England. She was an English scholar at Oxford in the 1950s. She worked for Drum Publications in South Africa for a short time and has lectured to adults in English. She has published *The Unlooked-For Season* (Scorpion Press 1960) which won the Gregory Award, *Rose in the Afternoon* (Dent 1974) which won the Cholmondeley Award, and *The Thinking Heart* (Secker and Warburg 1978).

Richard Kell was born in 1927 in County Cork. After five years in India, he was educated in Belfast and Dublin and graduated from Trinity College, Dublin. He is a senior lecturer at Newcastle upon Tyne Polytechnic. He has published poetry and criticism in various periodicals and several volumes of poems including *Fantasy Poets 35* (Fantasy Press 1957), *Control Tower* (Chatto 1962), *Differences* (Chatto 1969), *Heartwood* (Northern House 1978) and *Humours* (Ceolfrith Press 1978). Some of his orchestral compositions have been given professional performances and broadcast.

Frank Kelly was born in 1933 in Bradford and was educated at St Bede's Grammar School. He joined the army as a regular, and saw service in Egypt and Cyprus. He then had a variety of short-term jobs before settling down in the Civil Service. He was employed for several years in the Foreign Office but declined an overseas posting in order to return to Bradford. He was married in 1956 and has two sons (aged twelve and fifteen). His interests include politics and literature.

Averil King-Wilkinson lives in Lancashire. She studied English at Birkbeck College, London, and until recently was a lecturer in Further Education. She is a full-time writer of novels, stories and poems.

Lotte Kramer was born in Germany and came to England as a child. She has worked as a laundry hand, shop assistant, ladies' companion and has studied art and history of art in the evenings. She began writing poetry in 1970 since when her work has been published in magazines, newspapers and anthologies in England, the US and Canada.

Brenda Leckie studied biology at the Universities of East Anglia and Leeds, and works as a biochemist in Glasgow.

James Longwill was born in 1947 in Hartlepool and brought up in Middlesbrough. He is a school teacher and has published a pamphlet of poems, *A Man's Jacket* (Pig Press 1977).

Bette McArdle was born in Ayr in 1935 and now lives in Wick, Caithness. She studied art and worked as a freelance painter before turning to journalism. As well as appearing in magazines, her poems have been included in PEN and Arts Council anthologies and have been broadcast on BBC radio.

Medbh McGuckian was born in 1950 in Belfast where she now teaches English. Her poems haved been published in the *Irish Press, Fortnight* and other magazines: a selection is due to be published by the Blackstaff Press.

Jane McLaughlin was born near London in 1942 and studied at Oxford and Bryn Mawr College, Pennsylvania. She has worked as an administrator for Voluntary Service Overseas and now teaches English to foreigners. Her poems have been published in various magazines and in *New Poetry 2, 3 and 4*.

Mary Michaels was born in 1946. She studied at the University of Bristol and taught history of art for several years in Wolverhampton and in Philadelphia. She has given readings and broadcasts in England and America, and taught writing at the Arvon Foundation. Her work has appeared in magazines and anthologies including *New Studies Poets – 1* (Philadelphia 1974), and *New Poetry 3*. She was joint second prize winner at 1978 Stroud International Poetry Festival.

Anthony Mortimer was born in Birmingham and studied at Leeds University where he edited *Poetry and Audience*. He now holds the Chair of English at the University of Fribourg, Switzerland. He contributed to *New Poetry 2*, and his recent publications include a volume of verse translations from Petrarch's *Canzoniere*.

Norman Nicholson still lives in the house at Millom, Cumberland, where he was born in 1914. He has published six books of poems: the first, *Five Rivers* (Faber 1944) was awarded the first ever Heinemann Prize. He has also published four verse-plays, several volumes of literary criticism and on the topography and history of the Lake District and Cumbria. An autobiography, *Wednesday Early Closing*, was published by Faber in 1975. *The Shadow of Black Combe*, a pamphlet of fourteen poems, has recently been published by the Mid-Northumberland Arts Group, Ashington, Northumberland. He received a Cholmondeley Award in 1967, the Queen's Medal for Poetry in 1977 and an Arts Council bursary in the same year.

Dennis O'Driscoll was born in 1954. He studied Law at University College, Dublin. He is a regular reviewer of poetry, and a number of his poems have been broadcast and published.

Maggie O'Sullivan was born in Lincoln and has lived in London since 1969. She has read at various venues and on Radio London: her first collection of poems, *Tonetreks*, is awaiting publication.

Rodney Pybus was born in 1938 in Newcastle upon Tyne

and studied at the University of Cambridge. He lectured in English at Macquarie University, Sydney, and now lives and works in Cumbria. He has published three collections of poetry including *In Memoriam Milena* (Chatto & Windus 1973) which was awarded the Poetry Society's Alice Hunt Bartlett Prize; *Bridging Loans* (Chatto & Windus 1976); *At the Stone Junction* (Northern House, Newcastle 1978).

P. F. Ritchie was born in Sydney, Australia, in 1925. There he studied painting from 1946 to 1950 and held exhibitions in London in 1956 and 1958. His first novel was published in 1962 and he was awarded an Arts Council bursary in 1968. His publications include *The Protagonist* (1968) and *Confessions of a People Lover* (1969), two plays and a study of Australia.

Peter Robinson was born in 1953 in Salford, Lancashire. He went to school in Wigan and Liverpool and studied at the Universities of York and Cambridge. He is co-editor of *Perfect Bound,* is a painter and was co-ordinator of the Cambridge Poetry Festival. His poems, translations and reviews appear in various magazines: he has published *The Benefit Forms* (Lobby Press, Cambridge) and *Going Out to Vote* (Many Press, London). He is currently preparing a bilingual edition of poems by Pierre Reverdy.

Carol Rumens was born in Forest Hill, near Pear Tree Road. She now lives in the ornamental-cherry-tree suburb of Old Coulsdon. Her publications include *A Strange Girl in Bright Colours* (Quartet) and *A Necklace of Mirrors* (Ulsterman Publications).

Lawrence Sail was born in London in 1942. His poems have appeared in magazines and anthologies, including *New Poetry 1, 3* and *4,* and they have been broadcast on radio and television. His books of poetry include *Opposite Views* (J. M. Dent 1974), and *The Drowned River* (Mandeville Press 1978).

Valerie Sinason was born in 1946. She edits *Gallery* magazine and works with troubled children and is training in child psychotherapy. Her poems have appeared in *Ambit, Outposts, Contemporary Women Poets, New Poetry 1, 2* and *4.* She has performed her poems at fringe theatres, arts festivals etc.

A. H. Snow is a retired teacher living in his native Romford, Essex. He contributes to a variety of magazines and has broadcast several times. He is a prizewinner at the Stroud International Poetry Festival (1976) and St Albans (1974).

John Stathatos is a poet, writer and translator who was born in Athens in 1947. His poetry collections include *Log Book* (Oasis Books 1974), *Maps and Tracings* (Oxus Press 1976) and *In Passage* (Oxus Press 1979). He has also published several volumes of translations and a travel book, *The Long Drive,* was published by Pelham Books in 1978. He is currently editing the correspondence between George Seferis and Henry Miller, in between stints as a freelance journalist and photographer.

Alaric Sumner was born in 1952 and trained as an actor at East 15 Acting School. All his poems and visual work are intended for performance. He edits *words worth* magazine and his publications include *Songs of Nonsense & Experiment* (Zimmer Zimmer Press 1977) and *outski or There are Trees all over it* (in contralaboration with Richard Tabor, KMP K! 1979). His work has also appeared in *Alembic 7, Rawz 2½* and *Blueprint 5* and in other magazines.

James Sutherland-Smith was born in 1948 and has done various jobs from working with alcoholics to accountancy. He is now financial controller in a language school. His publications include *The Death of Orpheus* (Words Press 1976), and *Naming of the Arrow* (Salamander Imprint 1979). He has appeared in numerous anthologies and magazines and was a Gregory Award winner in 1978. He is Secretary of Poets' Workshop, editor of the magazine *Snail's Pace* and has taught under the W. H. Smith's *Poets in Schools* scheme.

George Szirtes was born in Budapest in 1948 and came to England in 1956. A selection of his work was published in *Poetry Introduction 4* (Faber 1978) and was recently followed by a volume of poetry *The Slant Door* (Secker and Warburg 1979). He now runs the Starwheel Press which produces anthologies of poems and etchings and has written a number of musical plays in collaboration with various composers.

Isobel Thrilling was born in Suffolk and brought up in a mining village in Yorkshire. She studied at the University of Hull. After operations that saved her eyesight, she began writing ten years ago. Her poems have been broadcast and published in *Tribune, Outposts, New Poetry* and various other magazines, including the *Royal Astronomical Society Quarterly Review*.

John Wakeman was born in 1928 in London and worked in public libraries there until 1957. He then worked at the Brooklyn Public Library, New York, and later became editor of a national professional magazine for librarians. Since that time he has edited *World Authors: 1950 to 1970* and has now completed its first supplement. His poems have appeared in *Ambit, Encounter, London Magazine* and others. His prose fables have appeared in the *New York Times* and the *Observer,* and his prose has been published in *Punch,* the *New Statesman* and other magazines.

Jack Winter is forty-three years old. He moved to England from Canada in 1976, and now lives at Lavenham, Suffolk. His fourteen plays have received professional production in Canada, the US and the UK as well as Europe. Another fourteen plays have been produced on radio; others have been produced on television and he has written two films. He has published two books of poetry: articles, poems and plays have appeared in many magazines and newspapers. Awards include Canada Council Fellowships, the Canadian Film Award and an Academy Award nomination. He holds the C. Day Lewis Fellowship as Resident Writer in Parliament Hill School, London.

'Z' recently returned to the Eastern Bloc after working in this country for some years. He left behind a collection of forty poems in English which have been edited by Paul Hyland.